Wins the 2025 Kentucky Derby

The Underdog Story That Shook Churchill Downs

Table of Contents

Introduction 1

Chapter 1 The Bloodline Less Traveled 3

    A Modest Pedigree 4

    Early Skepticism from Experts 5

    Why Bloodlines Still Matter 7

Chapter 2 A Team with a Dream 10

    The Unlikely Owner 11

    A Trainer with Heart, Not Hype 13

    Jockey in the Shadows 15

Chapter 3 Building a Champion from the Ground Up 18

    Training on Grit, Not Glory 19

    Small Track Lessons 21

    The Unseen Sacrifices 23

Chapter 4 Media, Money, and the Missing Spotlight 26

    Ignored by the Press 27

    Sponsors Who Walked Away 29

    Betting Odds and Public Opinion 31

Chapter 5 The Road to Churchill Downs 33

    Qualifying Against the Odds 34

    One Victory at a Time 36

    Skeptics Turn to Spectators 38

Chapter 6 Derby Day Drama 40

    The Paddock Pulse 41

    A Start Full of Surprises 43

    Weathering the Pressure 45

Chapter 7 The Race That Rewrote History 47

    The Opening Furlongs 49

    The Final Stretch... 52

    Crossing the Line 55

Chapter 8 After the Finish Line 59

    The Roar of the Crowd 61

    Media Reactions and Shockwaves 63

    Sovereignty's Name Echoes 66

Chapter 9 Redefining the Underdog 70

    What Makes an Underdog? 72

    Courage Over Cost 74

    A Legend in Hoofbeats 77

Chapter 10 Legacy in Motion 81

Changing the Narrative in Racing 83

New Fans, New Faith 86

Where Sovereignty Stands Today 89

Chapter 11 The Road Ahead 93

Training for the Future 95

Next Races and Challenges 98

Preparing for Retirement 101

Chapter 12 The Legacy of an Underdog 104

Impact on the Racing World 107

Inspiring Future Generations 110

The Myth of Perfection and the Power of Imperfection 113

Introduction

The Kentucky Derby isn't just a horse race—it's a living piece of American folklore. From the red roses draped over the winning steed to the thunderous energy of 150,000 fans packed into Churchill Downs, the event is a collision of tradition, adrenaline, and dreams. Each year, it draws the best of the best: horses with elite pedigrees, trainers with dynasties behind them, and owners backed by wealth and prestige. The Derby is more than a sporting event—it's a spectacle of legacy, a place where legends are born and myths are made. But every so often, something happens that cuts through the usual script—a story that reminds us why we fell in love with the sport in the first place.

In 2025, that story was Sovereignty.

As Derby Day approached, the 2025 racing season seemed to be following a familiar pattern. All eyes were on the big stables, and the media was buzzing over a handful of top contenders with million-dollar bloodlines and glowing track records. The weather forecast predicted sunshine and fast turf, setting the scene for what was expected to be a classic match-up of favorites. Analysts dissected training times, fan polls, and lineage charts. The betting boards leaned heavily toward the usual suspects, and Sovereignty—if mentioned at all—was an afterthought, barely a blip on the radar.

Yet, beneath the glitter of frontrunners and celebrity ownership, something extraordinary was brewing. A quiet murmur of interest had started to ripple through the lesser-known corners of the racetrack community. Some grooms, stable hands, and independent trainers whispered about a horse that didn't fit the mold but had something rare—grit. Sovereignty's performance in qualifying races showed steady improvement. There was no flash or fanfare, but there was something undeniable: heart. And sometimes, especially in a sport as unpredictable as horse racing, heart is what turns history on its head.

Sovereignty was not the horse you'd expect to see charging down the final stretch of Churchill Downs, let alone in first place. With a modest pedigree, limited funding, and a team of racing outsiders, he entered the 2025 Derby as a complete longshot. Owned by a first-time investor and trained by a veteran who hadn't seen a Derby in over a decade, Sovereignty was the quintessential underdog—unnoticed, underestimated, and unshaken.

But those who had spent time near him—who watched his stride, saw his focus, and sensed his fire—knew there was something different. He didn't carry the name recognition of a racing dynasty, but he carried something stronger: the weight of a dream and the power of perseverance. Sovereignty's name became a symbol, not just of rebellion against odds, but of the hope that in the world's grandest arenas, there's always room for the unexpected to rise.

The 2025 Kentucky Derby wasn't won by power or pedigree. It was won by a horse who refused to be overlooked—and a team who never stopped believing. This is their story.

Chapter 1
The Bloodline Less Traveled

In the high-stakes world of horse racing, pedigree is everything. A colt's lineage can determine its value before it ever sets hoof on a track. With stud fees reaching hundreds of thousands and bloodlines traced back to legendary champions, the sport is saturated with a belief that greatness must be inherited. So when Sovereignty emerged on the scene, many scoffed. His bloodline lacked star power. There were no Triple Crown winners in his ancestry, no record-breaking sires to boost confidence. On paper, he simply didn't belong.

The racing elite didn't hesitate to voice their doubts. Breeders, analysts, and commentators wrote him off as average at best—just another hopeful destined to fade before Derby Day. Even within casual racing circles, the consensus was clear: a horse without a powerful lineage might win small races, but he wouldn't stand a chance at Churchill Downs. The skepticism ran deep, and Sovereignty's team felt it at every turn—dismissive glances at auctions, ignored invites to elite training camps, and a noticeable lack of media interest.

Yet, as history has shown time and time again, the heart of a champion doesn't always lie in bloodlines. While the world placed its bets on breeding charts and family trees, Sovereignty was quietly building something more powerful: determination. His stride, his temperament, his growing strength—these weren't inherited from fame but forged through resilience and care. Bloodlines may set the stage, but they don't run the race. And as the 2025 Derby would prove, sometimes the most remarkable stories begin far from the spotlight of legacy.

A Modest Pedigree

In the world of Thoroughbred racing, pedigree is king. From the moment a foal is born, its bloodline determines its perceived value—and often its fate. Elite breeders pay six-figure stud fees to pair mares with proven sires, hoping to produce the next Triple Crown winner. Yearling sales catalogue pages are filled with detailed family trees tracing back to champions whose names have become legend: Secretariat, Man o' War, Seattle Slew. Buyers pore over these charts, convinced that greatness flows only through certain veins.

Sovereignty's lineage, by contrast, was humble. His sire—an easygoing stallion named Mariner's Hope—had shown glimpses of talent in minor stakes races but never captured a Grade I victory. His dam, River's Whisper, hailed from a modest regional breeding program in upstate New York. She won a handful of allowance races and proved a steady broodmare, but her foals were never considered blue-blood material. There were no Triple Crown champions, no record-setting speed demons in Sovereignty's immediate family—only solid, workmanlike runners who earned modest purses and returned to the breeding shed with little fanfare.

When Sovereignty went through the auction ring as a yearling, the bidding barely reached five figures. Observers shook their heads: why invest serious money in a horse whose ancestors had never raced on the sport's grandest stages? To many, he represented risk without reward—a pedigree too modest to dream on. The buyers who did show interest were small-scale owners and independent trainers, individuals more willing to take a chance on potential than pedigree. They saw in Sovereignty something the major stables overlooked: a well-balanced conformation, intelligent eyes, and a calm temperament—traits that sometimes matter more than illustrious bloodlines.

Behind the scenes, Sovereignty's connections quietly celebrated these very qualities. They believed that racing success depended not only on inherited speed but on heart, soundness, and the right human partnership. Mariner's Hope might not have been a superstar, but he passed on strong bone structure and a willing attitude. River's Whisper contributed stamina and an easy recovery after hard runs. Together, they produced a colt built for resilience more than flash—a horse whose pedigree whispered promise rather than shouted pedigree.

In an industry obsessed with lineage, Sovereignty's modest bloodline was a blemish on his résumé. Yet it was precisely this unassuming heritage—free from the weight of expectation—that allowed him to grow, learn, and surprise the racing world. In the chapters ahead, we'll see how this humble beginning became the foundation for a champion who would rewrite the story of what it means to come from nowhere and win everything.

Early Skepticism from Experts

Long before Sovereignty thundered down Churchill Downs' homestretch in 2025, racing experts had already rendered their verdict: he was a longshot at best. In an arena defined by pedigrees, purse earnings, and training connections, the colt's modest background was an immediate red flag to analysts, handicappers, and industry insiders. Their skepticism wasn't born of malice—rather, it was the product of decades spent decoding the patterns that separate champions from the also-rans. And in those patterns, Sovereignty simply didn't fit.

At the morning line unveiling, when oddsmakers set his initial Derby odds at 50-1, the murmurs began. Racing columnists penned dismissive previews: "Another name to skip on your ticket," one wrote, "unless you enjoy rooting for the improbable." Pundits on sports networks used Sovereignty as the punchline for underdog jokes. Their commentary focused less on his workouts or demeanor and more on what was absent: big-name owners, blue-blood lineage, and a string of graded stakes victories. To them, he was a convenient foil—a benchmark against which true contenders could shine.

In the paddock and at the barns, seasoned trainers and bloodstock agents echoed the sentiment. They noted his solid but unspectacular breeze times, his average two-year-old campaign, and the lack of buzz at the sales. One well-known trainer quipped that backing Sovereignty would be like betting on a pub league quarterback to win the Super Bowl. Another commented that while the colt had a "nice hop," he lacked the "killer turn of foot" that distinguishes elite racers. These off-hand remarks, relayed in whispers and hallway chatter, reinforced the public narrative: Sovereignty was unlikely to contend.

Even within his own team, uncertainty surfaced. When he shipped to Churchill Downs for the Derby undercard, stable staff overheard visiting trainers express surprise that he'd made the field at all. During morning workouts, rival grooms watched him lazily canter by, barely registering his presence. The local sportswriters, hungry for drama, cast him as the innocent bystander—an also-eligible who hit the gate after a late scratch. Their coverage was perfunctory, focusing instead on the headliners: the multimillion-dollar yearlings, the celebrity owners, the trainers with Triple Crown pedigrees.

Yet skepticism can be a double-edged sword. As experts dismissed Sovereignty, his team internalized the doubt as motivation. Each skeptical soundbite became fuel—proof that the colt's achievements to date had flown entirely under the radar. In workouts, his rider dug in harder; in stables, caretakers redoubled their attention to his diet, recovery, and conditioning. What experts saw as deficiencies—an unheralded record, lack of fanfare—became advantages. Sovereignty carried no burden of expectation; every stride was a surprise, every improvement a revelation.

By the eve of the Kentucky Derby, the chorus of doubt had reached its crescendo. Yet beneath the skepticism, a quieter truth was emerging: a horse unshaped by hype often runs freer, unfettered by the weight of pedigree and publicity. And in a race where legends fall as often as they rise, that freedom can be the greatest asset of all.

Why Bloodlines Still Matter

Throughout the sport of Thoroughbred racing, few factors attract as much attention—or spark as much debate—as bloodlines. While Sovereignty's modest pedigree and the doubts it inspired make for a compelling underdog narrative, it's important to understand why lineage remains a cornerstone of the industry.

Bloodlines still matter because they provide measurable insights into a horse's genetic potential, influence market dynamics, and shape training strategies—all of which can affect outcomes on the track.

First, pedigree charts offer tangible data about inherited traits. Over generations, breeders have identified stallions and mares whose offspring consistently demonstrate qualities such as speed, stamina, soundness, and temperament. These characteristics have heritable components—muscle fiber composition, cardiovascular capacity, bone density, and even behavioral tendencies. When a bloodline yields multiple champions, it signals that favorable genes are being passed along. Investors and trainers use this information to estimate a young horse's ceiling. While it's never a guarantee—environmental factors, training methods, and individual variation also play roles—it's a probabilistic edge in a sport where minute differences can decide multi-million-dollar purses.

Second, bloodlines drive the economics of racing. Horses descended from elite sires command premium prices at auction. Stud farms charge higher fees for champion stallions, creating a financial ecosystem built around lineage. This system attracts capital, funds top-tier training facilities, and underwrites the marketing machinery of the sport: high-profile sales, sponsorships, and media coverage. The result is a self-reinforcing cycle: top bloodlines generate revenue, which in turn supports further breeding and promotion of those lines. For the average owner or smaller stable, competing against that economic force can feel daunting—yet it also opens market niches for undervalued prospects like Sovereignty.

Third, knowledge of bloodlines informs training and management decisions. A pedigree indicating stamina influences race selection—longer routes rather than sprints—and conditions the training regimen to build aerobic endurance. Conversely, a lineage known for early speed might prompt connections to target juvenile stakes and tailor workouts for quick bursts. Even recovery protocols can be adjusted based on hereditary predispositions to certain injuries or sensitivities. In Sovereignty's case, his team recognized from his dam's side a tendency for robust recovery, allowing them to intensify conditioning without overtraining.

Yet bloodlines are not destiny. They represent probabilities, not certainties. Sovereignty's triumph demonstrated that factors like heart, training excellence, and strategic placement can overcome genetic expectations. His victory doesn't negate the value of pedigree; rather, it highlights that exceptional outcomes sometimes emerge from outside the established elite. In doing so, it reminds the racing world that while bloodlines remain a vital tool for prediction and investment, they are only one piece of a complex puzzle. The thrill of the sport endures because, every so often, a horse like Sovereignty gallops past the boundaries of expectation and into history.

Chapter 2
A Team with a Dream

In the world of elite horse racing, success often seems reserved for deep pockets and famous names. Yet behind every contender is a team driving the dream—and sometimes, the most unforgettable stories emerge when that team is anything but conventional. Chapter 2 introduces the unlikely coalition that rallied behind Sovereignty, transforming him from an overlooked yearling into a genuine Derby threat.

At the center of this coalition was an owner with nothing to prove and everything to gain. Unlike the established magnates whose stables brimmed with blue-blood prospects, this owner was a first-timer—drawn not by pedigree charts or pedigree parties, but by a simple passion for the sport and a belief in potential over pedigree. He invested savings rather than sponsorship deals, and he measured success not by headlines, but by the quiet progress he witnessed each morning at the track.

Standing beside him was a trainer whose reputation had long since slipped from the spotlight. Where marquee trainers chase media attention and pricey bloodstock, this trainer focused on fundamentals: conditioning, care, and understanding each horse's unique spirit. He saw in Sovereignty the same spark he'd once spotted in more celebrated runners, and he knew that genuine heart could outpace hype. Day by day, workout by workout, he nurtured the colt's strengths and shielded him from the cynicism echoing around the barns.

And then there was the jockey—a rider unknown outside niche racing circles, yet celebrated among insiders for an uncanny ability to coax peak performances from underdog mounts. He preferred the shadows to the spotlight, letting his skill speak through quiet confidence in the saddle. With no fanfare, he learned Sovereignty's rhythm, matched his stride, and prepared to guide him through the chaos of Derby Day.

Together, this unlikely owner, the devoted trainer, and the unheralded jockey formed a trio bound by belief. They had no guarantees—only conviction that heart, care, and unity could topple the giants of Churchill Downs. Their dream was audacious, but it was real. And as Sovereignty's story unfolded, it became clear that sometimes the most powerful forces in racing are forged not by fame or fortune, but by faith in each other.

The Unlikely Owner

In the high-stakes world of horse racing, ownership often comes with fame, wealth, and a lineage to match. It's a sport defined by elite families with generations of involvement and wealth that seems limitless. The typical racing owner is someone whose name is synonymous with the sport—someone who commands attention, commands influence, and commands victories. But Sovereignty's journey would not have followed this path. His story began with an unlikely owner, a man whose name wasn't etched in the pages of horse racing history—yet who would go on to play a pivotal role in writing a story that would reverberate through the sport.

This owner wasn't part of the establishment; in fact, he was the very antithesis of the typical horse racing mogul. A self-made entrepreneur from a small town with no prior connections to the horse racing world, he had never thought of investing in a racehorse until one casual trip to a local race in his mid-40s. That day, surrounded by the buzz of the track and the spirit of competition, something sparked in him. He was taken by the beauty and majesty of the horses, the power they seemed to hold, and the stories they represented. That was when the idea of ownership first entered his mind—not as a ticket to glory, but as a way to experience the sport from the inside, to be a part of something larger than himself.

With limited resources, he couldn't afford the top-tier horses that dominate the auction blocks. Instead, he found himself gravitating toward the underdogs—the horses that were dismissed, overlooked, or undervalued by the big players in the game. When Sovereignty came across his radar, the colt wasn't a glimmering race-bred prospect with the world's eyes on him. He was an overlooked yearling with a modest pedigree, a diamond in the rough. Despite the heavy skepticism surrounding Sovereignty, the owner saw something in him—an inner spark that seemed to promise more than the world was willing to see.

Without the safety net of a famous name or a massive bankroll, the owner made a calculated decision. He trusted his instincts, took a gamble, and purchased Sovereignty. But his purchase was not one made from the desire for instant glory or quick returns; it was a decision made out of passion for the sport, a desire to prove that dreams can come true even when the odds are stacked against you.

The journey was never about the trappings of success—it was about the love of the horse and the sport. He built his small team around that same passion, and with each step of Sovereignty's training, the owner grew more convinced that heart, determination, and belief in the underdog would take them further than anyone expected.

While the world doubted, this unlikely owner never faltered in his conviction. He became a testament to the idea that sometimes, those who have the least to prove can offer the most to the sport, rewriting what it means to own a racehorse—and in doing so, he helped Sovereignty become a champion.

A Trainer with Heart, Not Hype

In horse racing, the name of a trainer often carries as much weight as that of the horse itself. Trainers with impressive records, glossy resumes, and a fleet of elite horses are often in the media spotlight, celebrated as the architects of greatness. Their stables are packed with world-class athletes, and their reputations are built on a long list of victories. But for Sovereignty, the colt who defied all expectations, it was a trainer with no flashy reputation, no headlines, and no obsession with celebrity status who would prove to be his true catalyst.

This trainer had spent years on the fringes of the racing world, working quietly with horses that the mainstream racing establishment had long since written off. His name might not have been known to the casual observer, but within the circles of hard-working stable hands and fellow trainers, his expertise was respected and appreciated. He wasn't interested in the limelight or the quick fame that comes with training high-profile horses. Instead, he found his satisfaction in the day-to-day work of training, the small victories that don't always make the papers but form the foundation for success.

When Sovereignty arrived at his barn, the trainer saw something that others had missed: a horse full of potential but in need of patience and understanding. Sovereignty didn't have the pedigree or the accolades that many trainers coveted, but he had something more important: a willingness to learn, a strong constitution, and a quiet determination that couldn't be quantified by mere records or bloodlines. To the trainer, this was the essence of a champion, not flashy stats or high-profile backing.

Where other trainers might have dismissed Sovereignty as just another average horse, this trainer saw a puzzle that needed to be solved. He knew that horses like Sovereignty required something different—more than just a focus on speed or flashy performances. He took the time to understand Sovereignty's personality, his quirks, and his unique physicality. Instead of pushing the colt too hard early on, he allowed Sovereignty to grow into his own rhythm. The trainer didn't just focus on the races; he focused on Sovereignty as a horse—a living, breathing athlete with emotional needs, physical limits, and room for development.

His methods were rooted in heart, not hype. Sovereignty's training regimen was not built on flashy tactics or hard-driving schedules, but on care, consistency, and a deep understanding of the horse's needs. The trainer believed in allowing Sovereignty to learn at his own pace, reinforcing positive behaviors and slowly pushing him toward greater challenges as he matured. His belief was simple yet profound: that heart could always outlast hype, and consistency would eventually yield results far beyond what was expected.

As Sovereignty's success grew, it was clear that the trainer's commitment to the horse paid off. While others might have dismissed Sovereignty as a longshot, the trainer knew what the colt was capable of. He nurtured him with a steady hand, always believing in his heart that Sovereignty could rise above the doubters and prove the world wrong. And as Sovereignty began to find success, it became clear that this trainer had played a quiet but essential role in shaping him into the champion he would become. In a world dominated by the high-profile and the high-budget, this trainer showed that heart, patience, and respect for the horse were sometimes the greatest assets of all.

Jockey in the Shadows

In a sport that thrives on spectacle, where victory often feels synonymous with fame, the jockey who rides the race remains, in many cases, the unsung hero. The media gravitates toward trainers, owners, and horses, leaving the jockey in the shadows, a figure often overlooked despite the pivotal role they play. Sovereignty's unlikely victory at the 2025 Kentucky Derby, however, would not have been possible without the quiet, yet brilliant, performance of his jockey—an individual whose skill was as much about understanding the horse as it was about knowing the art of riding itself.

Sovereignty's jockey was far from the celebrity riders who frequently dominate headlines. He wasn't a household name, nor did he possess the high-profile sponsorship deals that most top jockeys boasted. In fact, he was the kind of rider who preferred to avoid the spotlight. While other jockeys flashed their trophies and graced the covers of magazines, he stayed out of the public eye, letting his riding speak for itself. His reputation was built not on flashy performances, but on his uncanny ability to get the best out of horses that were often deemed "unlikely" by the racing world.

In the case of Sovereignty, this jockey understood that the colt was not just another entry in a field of well-bred horses. Sovereignty's modest pedigree and lack of hype meant that he didn't have the same established pattern of success that other Derby horses had. The jockey knew that he needed to form a bond with Sovereignty, to get a true sense of the colt's stride, rhythm, and personality before they could even think about tackling the big race. Every workout, every quiet morning on the track, was an opportunity for him to learn the nuances of Sovereignty's movement.

The jockey wasn't concerned with the fast headlines or the media circus that swirled around the big Derby names. His focus was unwavering: he was determined to be the calm force that would help Sovereignty find his true potential. He worked tirelessly with the colt, building trust, and ensuring that Sovereignty's confidence was nurtured at every turn. He didn't push too hard; instead, he guided Sovereignty through every race and workout with a careful, patient hand—knowing that the colt needed time to grow into the athlete he was becoming.

When it came time for the Kentucky Derby, the jockey's quiet determination paid off. As the race unfolded, he stayed cool under pressure, never rushing, never panicking. He knew the right moments to push and the right moments to hold back, patiently guiding Sovereignty through the field. The jockey's connection to Sovereignty was almost telepathic; he could feel when the colt was ready to make his move and when he needed more time to recover. It was this deep understanding of the horse that allowed him to navigate the chaos of the Derby with precision, ultimately guiding Sovereignty to victory.

In the end, Sovereignty's jockey remained in the shadows, letting the colt's win and the team's success take center stage. But the reality is that without his dedication, his steady hand, and his intimate knowledge of Sovereignty, the colt's improbable rise to victory would not have been possible. The jockey may not have craved fame or recognition, but his skill and unwavering belief in his horse was the secret ingredient that turned Sovereignty from an overlooked contender into the Derby champion.

Chapter 3
Building a Champion from the Ground Up

Building a champion is never as glamorous as it seems on race day. For every Derby winner that crosses the finish line in a blaze of glory, there are countless hours spent in quiet training, far from the media spotlight. Sovereignty's journey to victory in the 2025 Kentucky Derby was no different. It was built on raw determination, a refusal to accept defeat, and an unwavering commitment to developing a horse who was as much a testament to hard work as to natural talent.

The story of Sovereignty's rise was not written in headlines but in the small, uncelebrated moments that took place on the training grounds. While the world's eyes were focused on the big stables and pedigrees, Sovereignty's team was dedicated to training him with a focus on grit, not glory. They knew that true champions are forged in the quiet hours before the race, when the real work happens behind the scenes. Sovereignty wasn't trained for fame, but for perseverance. His success was never guaranteed, and every stride he took toward greatness came through lessons in resilience, discipline, and heart.

Training on small tracks and away from the distractions of the big leagues, Sovereignty learned the value of persistence. Each workout was an opportunity to refine his strength and endurance, to hone his mind and body for the challenges ahead. But what the public didn't see were the unseen sacrifices—those moments when Sovereignty's team poured everything into his development, sacrificing time, resources, and comfort for the chance at something greater.

In this chapter, we explore how Sovereignty was built from the ground up, focusing not on his pedigree or potential, but on the hard-earned qualities that would turn him into a Derby champion. It was a process of slow and steady growth, guided by a team that believed in him when few others did.

Training on Grit, Not Glory

In the world of Thoroughbred racing, where glory often takes center stage, it's easy to forget that true champions are built on grit, not just speed or pedigree. Sovereignty's rise to the 2025 Kentucky Derby wasn't a tale of instant success or a meteoric rise to fame—it was a story of unwavering determination, tireless effort, and the belief that heart could carry a horse further than any glamorous bloodline.

Unlike many of the horses that dominate the spotlight with their flashy performances, Sovereignty wasn't groomed for fame. From the moment he entered the training barn, it was clear that his journey would be different. There were no grand expectations placed on his shoulders, no sponsorship deals or media buzz. Instead, Sovereignty's team took a unique approach, focusing not on the promise of immediate results, but on long-term growth and development. His training was designed to build strength and resilience, qualities that would serve him well when the pressure was at its highest.

The focus was always on the process, not the end result. His training sessions weren't about showing off to the crowd or impressing the media. They were about pushing through physical and mental barriers, fostering a work ethic that would stand the test of time. Sovereignty's daily routines included long, grueling workouts designed to increase his stamina and endurance. While other horses may have been trained with an eye toward flashy performances, Sovereignty's team was more concerned with shaping him into a horse capable of withstanding the rigorous demands of the Derby.

Training wasn't limited to what Sovereignty could achieve on the track—it also focused on building his mental toughness. There were no shortcuts in his training; every workout, every lap around the track, was an opportunity to reinforce the lessons of perseverance. Whether it was navigating tight turns or learning to push through exhaustion, Sovereignty's team emphasized the importance of consistency and resilience over instantaneous glory.

Every session brought new challenges and obstacles. Yet Sovereignty proved himself time and time again. He may not have been the most naturally gifted horse, but he was willing to fight through fatigue, pain, and doubt. His trainers never let up, knowing that the road to success was paved not with ease, but with hard work.

As Sovereignty's conditioning improved, so did his confidence. It became clear that while others might have been born with the promise of speed or power, Sovereignty's true strength lay in his ability to keep going when others would falter. He wasn't trained for quick success; he was trained for endurance, for resilience, for the long haul. And when the Kentucky Derby finally arrived, it was that grit—built in the quiet, unsung hours of training—that would propel him across the finish line.

Small Track Lessons

In horse racing, many of the sport's most celebrated horses are trained on the grandest tracks, under the watchful eyes of prestigious trainers and high-profile stables. These tracks are often seen as the proving grounds, where future champions are molded and polished before they make their mark on the biggest stages. But for Sovereignty, the journey to greatness was shaped not by the glamour of large, renowned tracks, but by the quiet discipline of smaller, less-traveled courses where his true potential began to take form.

The small tracks, tucked away from the media's gaze, were where Sovereignty's foundation was built. These tracks, with their simpler facilities and less glamorous surroundings, became a place for Sovereignty to learn the ropes without the distractions and expectations that come with fame. Here, he wasn't competing against the top-tier colts bred for speed and perfection. Instead, Sovereignty faced horses of varying abilities, allowing him to grow at his own pace, developing his skills in a more intimate environment.

At these smaller tracks, Sovereignty learned crucial lessons that would set him apart from his more celebrated competitors. His trainers focused on refining his stride, teaching him how to navigate turns with precision and how to build his stamina without overextending himself. Unlike the big, sprawling courses where every mistake was magnified and scrutinized, Sovereignty had the chance to make mistakes and learn from them in a less pressured environment. The importance of these small track lessons cannot be overstated—here, Sovereignty was allowed to develop the resilience and confidence that would later become his trademark.

For Sovereignty, small tracks meant learning the importance of consistency. Each lap around a smaller, less intricate track allowed him to fine-tune his timing, adjusting his pace in a way that helped him understand his limits and how to push past them. These early training sessions focused on building a relationship between Sovereignty and his rider, one grounded in trust and patience. He wasn't expected to perform at the level of the seasoned horses racing on grander tracks; instead, he was learning the fundamentals, gaining the experience that would prepare him for the big leagues.

The smaller tracks also provided Sovereignty with the time and space to develop his mental strength. On these tracks, he wasn't just racing against other horses—he was learning to race against himself, pushing his boundaries with each run. The lack of constant media attention and celebrity hype gave him the opportunity to simply focus on the task at hand: becoming a stronger, more capable racehorse.

These small track lessons weren't just about training physically; they were about creating a horse with heart, a horse that could dig deep when the race got tough. Sovereignty learned that the road to victory wasn't always about competing in the biggest races, but about mastering the basics first. By the time he made his way to the grander tracks and the bigger races, he was equipped with more than just speed—he had the resilience, patience, and mental toughness needed to succeed on the grandest stage of all.

The Unseen Sacrifices

Behind every champion, there are sacrifices that often go unseen—quiet, behind-the-scenes efforts made not for recognition but for the belief in something greater. For Sovereignty, the path to the 2025 Kentucky Derby was shaped by countless unseen sacrifices made by his team, who poured their time, energy, and resources into him long before he ever made headlines. These sacrifices were not just about training; they were about commitment, belief, and the willingness to invest in a dream that seemed improbable to most.

For Sovereignty's owner, the sacrifices began long before the colt was even in full training. As a first-time racehorse owner, his investment in Sovereignty wasn't just financial—it was personal. With limited resources, the owner had to forgo luxuries that many in the racing world take for granted. There were no lavish trips to international breeding farms, no lavish perks for his team, and no big-budget campaigns to market Sovereignty's name. Every dollar spent on Sovereignty was carefully considered, invested into his care, his training, and his development. The owner chose to forgo personal luxuries to make sure that Sovereignty had every chance to succeed, sacrificing the comfort of financial security in the hope that his horse would defy the odds.

For the trainer, the sacrifices were emotional and physical. This was a man who had already spent decades in the sport, long past the point of seeking fame or accolades. His career had seen both triumphs and disappointments, yet when he took on Sovereignty, it felt different. There were no guarantees, no promises of success. His training sessions were long and grueling, often stretching late into the evening after other horses had long gone back to their stables. He put aside personal time, missing family events, and made personal sacrifices in terms of his own health and well-being to ensure that Sovereignty was receiving the attention and care he needed. There were times when he questioned whether his efforts were worth it, as the skepticism around Sovereignty's prospects persisted. But the trainer never wavered, knowing that every early morning workout, every moment of extra attention, was building the foundation for a potential champion.

Then there were the unseen sacrifices of the support staff—the grooms, the veterinarians, the exercise riders, and the stable hands. These individuals worked tirelessly behind the scenes, ensuring Sovereignty was physically prepared for every race. They were the first ones at the barn in the morning and the last to leave at night. Their sacrifices often went unnoticed by the public, but without them, Sovereignty would not have had the chance to become the horse he was. Their commitment to his care was unwavering, from monitoring his nutrition to ensuring his recovery after long workouts. They were the quiet heroes of Sovereignty's journey, giving their time, expertise, and dedication without seeking anything in return.

Lastly, there were the sacrifices made by Sovereignty himself. He didn't have the luxury of choosing when to rest or when to push his body further. He ran through pain, fatigue, and doubt. The long hours in the training barn, the repetitive drills, the pressure to succeed—all were part of the sacrifices he made on the road to greatness. Sovereignty's journey was one of resilience, and though the world may have seen the glory of his final victory, it was built on the countless unseen sacrifices of those who believed in him from the start.

These sacrifices were not visible in the headlines or the glossy photos that followed Sovereignty's Derby win, but they were the backbone of his success. They were the quiet investments in time, energy, and faith that made all the difference when it mattered most.

Chapter 4
Media, Money, and the Missing Spotlight

In the world of horse racing, where media attention, sponsorships, and betting odds often shape a horse's reputation before it even crosses the finish line, Sovereignty's journey to the 2025 Kentucky Derby was defined by what he didn't have—publicity, backing, and attention. As the racing industry focused on the well-known horses with glamorous pedigrees and high-profile trainers, Sovereignty's story was largely ignored by the press, his potential largely overlooked by sponsors, and his odds long in the betting markets. He was, in many ways, an outsider—unnoticed, underestimated, and absent from the hype that normally surrounds Derby contenders.

The media, fixated on the usual favorites, barely mentioned Sovereignty's name. His underdog status was a narrative that didn't make headlines, nor did it generate the kind of buzz that the sport's biggest stars could stir. Sponsors, who flocked to the more glamorous names, turned their backs on Sovereignty, failing to see the potential that his team believed in so strongly. Meanwhile, the betting world—focused on pedigree and prior success—set Sovereignty's odds so high that to back him seemed like pure folly.

Despite this, Sovereignty's team was undeterred. In a world that thrives on visibility, they knew that the lack of attention could work in their favor. The media ignored him, the sponsors walked away, and the odds remained stacked against him—but that only added to the fire that would eventually propel Sovereignty toward his impossible victory. This chapter explores the forces of media, money, and public opinion that tried to define Sovereignty's story before he could even run his race, and how his team used those very obstacles as fuel to prove everyone wrong.

Ignored by the Press

In the world of horse racing, media coverage plays a critical role in shaping a horse's reputation and public perception. For the big names—the pedigreed stallions, the celebrity owners, the high-profile trainers—the press is quick to shower them with attention, creating a narrative long before the race even begins. For Sovereignty, however, media attention was a luxury he could only dream of. As the 2025 Kentucky Derby approached, his name was scarcely mentioned in the racing news, overshadowed by more glamorous horses who were already being groomed as the main contenders.

The press was obsessed with the favorites: horses bred from million-dollar bloodlines, horses with established trainers, and those with records of impressive wins at prestigious events. Articles were written about the star horses—highlighting their victories, their sponsors, and their odds. Television segments were dedicated to their preparation, showcasing them at the track with cameras capturing every stride and every breath. These horses were media darlings, receiving not just coverage but also endorsements, merchandise deals, and even social media buzz. In the eyes of the press, the race was already decided.

Meanwhile, Sovereignty remained largely invisible. Few racing journalists thought him worthy of mention, dismissing him as a mere afterthought in a field of heavyweights. Articles that should have spotlighted his underdog story, his training progress, or his potential remained absent. He wasn't a part of the glamorous narrative the media sought to create. The press didn't care to cover his humble beginnings, the long hours of training in smaller tracks, or the quiet belief his team had in him. Sovereignty was reduced to a name on the list of entries, nothing more than a footnote in a race dominated by the elite.

This lack of media attention wasn't just an oversight—it was a statement. To the press, Sovereignty wasn't a story worth telling. They saw no spectacle in him, no drama, no marketable narrative to draw in fans or sponsors. But this, in a strange way, became a blessing for Sovereignty and his team. As the media focused on the well-known contenders, no one was watching him closely. There were no distractions, no added pressure from reporters constantly in his face, no intrusive questions about his chances of winning. Sovereignty was left to train in peace, unnoticed by the very industry that would soon find itself stunned by his victory.

In the face of being ignored by the press, Sovereignty's team continued to work quietly, undeterred by the lack of media validation. They knew that the real story wasn't being told in the headlines—it was unfolding on the track, away from the cameras. The media's blind spot would soon become one of the greatest stories in racing history, proving that sometimes, the most powerful victories come from the most overlooked corners of the sport.

Sovereignty's true potential would be revealed not through media coverage, but through grit, perseverance, and an unwavering belief in the underdog.

Sponsors Who Walked Away

In the world of horse racing, sponsorships are essential to the success of both horses and their teams. They provide not only financial support but also the visibility and marketing muscle that can turn a horse into a household name. From high-end brands to corporate giants, the sponsors that attach their names to a horse's racing campaign do so with an eye on the potential for return on investment. In most cases, this means signing on the horses that already have a proven track record of success or come from prestigious bloodlines. For Sovereignty, the story was quite different—his underdog status and lack of media hype led many sponsors to walk away.

As Sovereignty's team worked tirelessly to prepare for the 2025 Kentucky Derby, they faced a significant challenge: a lack of sponsorship. In an industry where top-tier horses are often backed by major brands looking to capitalize on success, Sovereignty's lack of pedigree and media presence made him an unappealing candidate for potential sponsors. While other contenders, with their glamorous pedigrees and celebrity owners, were offered endorsement deals and marketing campaigns, Sovereignty found himself on the outside looking in. No major brands were knocking on his door. No national campaigns were being planned around his name. The press had largely ignored him, and with no media buzz or flashy appearances to attach themselves to, sponsors simply walked away.

Some sponsors turned their backs on Sovereignty outright, dismissing him as a longshot with little potential for return. The idea of backing a horse with no immediate fame or record of high-profile victories didn't align with their brand strategy. They wanted a safe bet—one that would shine in the media, pull in attention, and lead to increased sales and exposure. Sovereignty didn't fit that mold. His story wasn't about immediate success or guaranteed wins. He was a horse with a modest background, competing with more decorated horses whose media profiles were already established. The sponsors who walked away believed they were investing in the future of a horse who simply didn't have the marketable appeal to justify the expense.

Yet this very lack of sponsorship proved to be a hidden blessing for Sovereignty's team. With no outside financial interests or media campaigns pushing for quick results, Sovereignty was allowed to grow at his own pace. There were no lofty expectations from sponsors demanding instant results or flashy performances. His team was free to focus entirely on his development, training him for long-term success without the added pressure of appeasing big-name backers. This absence of sponsorship gave Sovereignty the space to be himself, to train with patience and build his strength, without the looming demands of commercial success clouding his progress.

As the 2025 Kentucky Derby approached, Sovereignty's team, though disappointed by the lack of sponsorship support, had one thing that no sponsor could buy: the freedom to work solely toward their goal. The sponsorships that walked away allowed them to focus purely on the work at hand, and when Sovereignty crossed the finish line in an improbable victory, it wasn't because of a lucrative deal with a corporate sponsor—it was because of the unrelenting effort, belief, and determination of the team behind him. While sponsors may have turned away, Sovereignty's victory was proof that sometimes the greatest triumphs come when you're not tied to the expectations of the world, but to your own sense of purpose.

Betting Odds and Public Opinion

In horse racing, the betting odds are often seen as a reflection of a horse's potential to win, shaping public opinion and influencing how races are viewed. These odds are heavily influenced by pedigree, past performances, trainer reputation, and media coverage. Sovereignty, with his modest background and underdog status, was given long odds that made him an unlikely contender in the eyes of the public. As the Kentucky Derby approached in 2025, the betting world—and the public—had already written him off.

The odds against Sovereignty were astronomical. According to bookmakers, he was nothing more than a filler in a race dominated by horses with established pedigrees and reputations. His odds started at 50-1, a reflection of the general belief that, despite his training and effort, he stood little chance against the race's heavy favorites. The public opinion mirrored these odds. To most, Sovereignty was a curiosity at best—a horse whose participation in the Derby was more about filling out the field than about actually contending for the win. His name was barely mentioned in discussions about potential Derby winners. Instead, the attention was focused on the pedigrees, records, and hype surrounding other horses.

The betting world thrives on predictions, numbers, and trends, and in this case, the numbers overwhelmingly pointed to Sovereignty as a non-contender. Bettors put their money on the familiar horses, the ones whose histories were rich with wins and whose trainers and owners were known throughout the industry. Public opinion followed suit, as people placed bets not on potential, but on reputation. The general public, driven by the media's portrayal of the race, believed that the Derby was already decided — that the favorites were guaranteed to claim victory. Sovereignty was simply an afterthought, a mere footnote in a race dominated by the more glamorous entrants.

Yet, these long odds became part of the very story that would make Sovereignty's victory so extraordinary. The betting odds didn't just represent his chances—they represented the collective underestimation of his abilities. Every bettor who chose the favorites over him added to the mountain of skepticism Sovereignty and his team had to overcome. But these odds, set against him, only fueled his determination. The lack of public belief became something to prove, not just to the world, but to himself.

When Sovereignty crossed the finish line first in the Derby, it was more than just an upset—it was a direct challenge to the established system of predictions and perceptions. The betting odds had been wrong, the public opinion misguided, and the critics silenced. Sovereignty's victory shattered the notion that success in racing was determined by pedigree and media hype. Instead, it showed that true champions are often the ones who are overlooked and underestimated, waiting for the moment when they can defy the odds and rewrite the narrative.

Chapter 5
The Road to Churchill Downs

The road to Churchill Downs, the hallowed ground where the Kentucky Derby unfolds, is never an easy one. For Sovereignty, the journey was anything but traditional. His path to the 2025 Kentucky Derby was filled with challenges, doubts, and countless skeptics who questioned his ability to compete against horses with more prestigious pedigrees and greater financial backing. But Sovereignty's story wasn't about following the beaten path—it was about carving out his own way, defying expectations, and proving that determination, heart, and grit could lead to greatness, even in the face of overwhelming odds.

Qualifying for the Kentucky Derby is a feat in itself, and for Sovereignty, it was no different. He wasn't an immediate favorite, nor did he have the kind of fanfare or recognition that many of the other horses enjoyed. His journey to qualifying was a story of perseverance and steady improvement, showing that even when things didn't seem to go his way, Sovereignty never backed down. Each race, each qualifier, and each step towards Churchill Downs was a victory of its own. It wasn't just about winning; it was about proving that he had the heart to continue fighting, despite the hurdles he faced along the way.

As Sovereignty continued to defy expectations, his story began to shift the narrative around him. The skeptics who once dismissed him as an underdog started to take notice. What had once seemed impossible was beginning to look more like a reality. By the time Sovereignty entered the Kentucky Derby, the world had begun to see him not just as an outsider, but as a contender. His journey was more than just about racing—it was a testament to the power of resilience and belief, and the road ahead promised even more surprises for this unlikely champion.

Qualifying Against the Odds

Sovereignty's road to qualifying for the 2025 Kentucky Derby was far from smooth, and every step was a testament to his resilience and determination. Unlike some of the more well-known horses, whose breeding and financial backing placed them on a fast track to the Derby, Sovereignty's journey was defined by overcoming obstacles and proving himself time and time again. Qualifying against the odds was not just about winning races—it was about defying expectations, silencing the skeptics, and showing that a horse without the most illustrious pedigree could still make it to the biggest stage in racing.

From the beginning, Sovereignty faced doubts from many in the racing world. Despite his impressive performances on smaller tracks, he was often dismissed as a long shot. His modest bloodlines, combined with the lack of a heavy-hitting owner or trainer, led many to write him off as an underdog—one whose chances of even qualifying for the Kentucky Derby were slim. But Sovereignty was not the kind of horse to be deterred by such assessments. Each race he entered, he raced with everything he had, slowly proving that he had the heart and ability to compete with the best.

The challenge of qualifying for the Kentucky Derby is immense, and for Sovereignty, it meant consistently outperforming expectations in various prep races. The Derby requires not only skill and speed but also consistency and stamina over multiple races. In each qualifying race, Sovereignty faced fierce competition from horses with much more impressive resumes and a pedigree that seemed to guarantee success. Yet, Sovereignty consistently outran them, displaying a level of grit and tenacity that set him apart. The press and fans who had once ignored him began to take notice of the horse who kept defying the odds.

Qualifying for the Derby itself requires a horse to accumulate points through various prep races, and Sovereignty did so with calculated precision. Each race was a stepping stone, bringing him closer to the ultimate prize. There were setbacks, of course—close races where Sovereignty came in second or faced tough competition. But every time he lost, he came back stronger, showing more determination and drive than before. His trainer, jockey, and owner all worked tirelessly to ensure that Sovereignty was in the best condition possible for every race, understanding that his journey wasn't just about speed, but about mental fortitude.

By the time Sovereignty earned his spot at Churchill Downs, he had already proven that he was more than just a horse with potential—he was a competitor, capable of taking on the best. Qualifying against the odds was not just about physical preparation; it was about mental strength, belief, and the unwavering support of a team that saw his potential when others didn't. Sovereignty had gone from being a forgotten horse to a legitimate contender for the Kentucky Derby. His qualification was more than a race result; it was a triumph of determination, showing the racing world that sometimes, it's the underdog who has the most to prove.

One Victory at a Time

Sovereignty's journey to the 2025 Kentucky Derby was defined by the phrase "one victory at a time." While his ultimate goal was the Derby itself, each race he entered along the way was a crucial step in proving to himself and the world that he belonged among the elite. These victories, often hard-fought and surrounded by skepticism, were more than just race wins; they were markers of his growth, resilience, and determination. Sovereignty's success came not from a single race, but from the accumulation of moments where he defied the odds, overcame obstacles, and proved his worth, one victory at a time.

From the outset, Sovereignty was seen as an underdog. His pedigree, while respectable, was not on par with the horses that dominated the racing world, and many believed that his lack of financial backing and connections would limit his potential. But Sovereignty's team, knowing that the road to the Kentucky Derby would require a series of victories, approached each race with careful strategy, focusing not just on winning, but on learning, improving, and building momentum.

Each victory in the prep races was a crucial step toward his goal. These were not easy wins. Sovereignty faced stiff competition from horses with bigger reputations, better breeding, and more substantial financial resources. Yet, Sovereignty managed to prove time and time again that heart, drive, and preparation could compete with the wealth of pedigree and sponsorship. Whether it was a close victory, a hard-fought race, or a tactical win, each one added points to his qualification tally and strengthened the belief that he could one day challenge for the Derby crown.

The process of winning was methodical, and Sovereignty's victories were often marked by strategic moves that highlighted his growth as a racer. In one race, he might show an incredible burst of speed to pull ahead in the final stretch, while in another, he might demonstrate an unshakable resolve, digging deep to hold onto his position despite mounting pressure. It wasn't just about winning for Sovereignty—it was about learning how to win, refining his strategies with each race.

By taking each victory as a building block, Sovereignty's journey became a story of gradual growth. The victories weren't just about claiming titles or points for the Derby—they were proof of Sovereignty's ability to adapt, to overcome, and to rise above. With each race, his team honed in on areas for improvement, strengthening his weaknesses and fine-tuning his strengths. The wins weren't just the result of natural ability; they were the culmination of hard work, mental toughness, and a willingness to improve, even when things seemed difficult.

Each race was a step forward, and with every victory, Sovereignty proved that he was more than just an underdog—he was a contender. One victory at a time, Sovereignty dismantled the doubts and built a foundation that would carry him all the way to Churchill Downs. His journey wasn't just about a single triumph; it was about the accumulation of victories that showcased his perseverance and growth, culminating in the moment when he would step onto the grandest stage of all—the Kentucky Derby.

Skeptics Turn to Spectators

As Sovereignty made his way through the ranks toward the 2025 Kentucky Derby, one of the most remarkable aspects of his journey was the shift in perception about his abilities. From the moment he entered the racing scene, Sovereignty had been viewed with skepticism. Many in the industry and the media dismissed him as a long shot, an underdog with little chance of making it to the prestigious Derby. His modest bloodlines, combined with his lack of financial backing and high-profile connections, led many to believe that his success would be limited and that the spotlight would ultimately shine on more pedigreed, well-funded horses.

However, with each race, Sovereignty began to prove the skeptics wrong. At first, his victories were met with surprise and disbelief. Many expected him to fade into the background, never able to compete with horses bred for success. But Sovereignty continued to silence his doubters, winning races one by one and securing the points he needed to qualify for the Derby. With every victory, his skeptics were forced to reassess their opinions of him. What started as a few raised eyebrows turned into full-fledged respect as Sovereignty not only qualified for the Kentucky Derby but did so by consistently outperforming horses with more prestigious pedigrees.

The turning point came when Sovereignty not only qualified for the Derby but also began to attract attention from a broader audience. As his story of perseverance, resilience, and determination unfolded, people began to take notice—not just of his victories, but of the journey he had taken to get there. The very skeptics who had once dismissed him as a non-contender found themselves watching his every move, now intrigued by the horse who had defied expectations at every turn.

By the time Sovereignty entered the gates of Churchill Downs for the 2025 Kentucky Derby, those who had once doubted him were no longer in the background. They had become spectators, watching in awe as Sovereignty, the horse who had been counted out from the beginning, stood on the precipice of greatness. His journey had turned his skeptics into admirers, and his victory would ultimately prove that, in the world of horse racing, even the most unlikely horses could capture the hearts of millions and take their place among the legends of the sport.

Sovereignty's rise from skepticism to admiration symbolized the essence of his career—defying expectations at every step. His journey wasn't just about proving others wrong; it was about showing that perseverance, heart, and belief in one's abilities could turn the most unlikely contender into a champion. The skeptics who once doubted him were now among the most vocal supporters, applauding his success and acknowledging that they had witnessed a story that would go down in history as one of the greatest underdog tales in horse racing.

Chapter 6
Derby Day Drama

Derby Day is a spectacle unlike any other, where anticipation, excitement, and nerves combine to create an atmosphere of pure adrenaline. As the horses parade into the paddock, the energy is palpable—an entire year's worth of training, hope, and dreams about to unfold. For Sovereignty, this day was the culmination of a journey that had seen him ignored by the press, overlooked by sponsors, and dismissed by the betting world. But now, as he stood in the paddock with the eyes of the world upon him, he was no longer just the underdog. He was about to prove that the odds could be beaten, the critics silenced, and the impossible made possible.

In this chapter, we delve into the drama of Derby Day, beginning with the palpable pulse of the paddock as the horses prepare for the race of a lifetime. Sovereignty, calm and collected in the midst of the chaos, exuded an unspoken confidence that set him apart from his competitors. The quiet determination he had developed over months of hard training was about to be tested in a way that no small track could replicate. As the gates opened, Sovereignty's team held their breath, knowing that everything they had worked for had led to this one moment.

The start of the race would be full of surprises—both expected and unexpected. Sovereignty wasn't supposed to be a contender, but as the field jostled for position, he began to make his move. The pressure of the Derby, with its thousands of fans and the weight of history, could be overwhelming for any horse, but Sovereignty proved himself ready to weather it all. As the race unfolded, so too did the story of a champion being born under the bright lights of Churchill Downs.

The Paddock Pulse

The paddock on Kentucky Derby Day is a place of controlled chaos—a space where horses are readied, owners and trainers nervously pace, and the energy of anticipation radiates through the crowd. It is here, moments before the race begins, that the true pulse of the Derby can be felt. Sovereignty, standing calmly among the elite horses of the field, was an anomaly in this electric environment. While the famous thoroughbreds fidgeted with the nervous energy of the moment, Sovereignty stood composed, a quiet strength emanating from him. His calm demeanor was a stark contrast to the anxiety buzzing around him, and it was clear that he was ready for something extraordinary.

The paddock is more than just a staging area—it is a place where the horses are mentally prepared for the race ahead. Jockeys adjust their silks, grooms make final checks, and owners exchange glances filled with both hope and doubt. For Sovereignty, this was a space where the weight of expectation had not yet settled upon him. Unlike the media darlings and favorites, Sovereignty wasn't under the same scrutiny. There were no flashbulbs popping in his face, no reporters crowding around him for quotes. Instead, he was allowed to focus inward, absorbing the gravity of the moment without the added distractions of the spotlight.

As Sovereignty stood in the paddock, his team watched him closely, noting his body language—calm, focused, ready. His trainer, the one who had nurtured him from a modest yearling to this moment, could hardly hide the pride in his eyes. There was no fanfare around Sovereignty, no media circus, but in the calm before the storm, there was a deep understanding between the horse and his team: they had put in the work, and now it was time to see it all come to fruition.

Meanwhile, the paddock was full of familiar faces—owners whose horses were heavily favored, trainers known for their Derby pedigree, and jockeys who were already household names. They were all here, and Sovereignty was just another name on the list. Yet, as the horses were led to the starting gates, there was a sense that something was different about Sovereignty. His presence in the paddock was quiet yet powerful—he wasn't consumed by the surrounding hype, and that alone made him stand out from the rest. Sovereignty wasn't part of the media circus or the betting excitement; he was here simply to race, and that singular purpose would soon be his greatest strength.

As the final moments in the paddock ticked down and Sovereignty was led out to the starting gates, the world around him swirled in a haze of noise and motion. But for Sovereignty, there was only focus. The paddock pulse—the anticipation, the energy— was something he absorbed, not as a weight, but as a signal that his time had come. As the horses lined up, Sovereignty was poised, ready to break free from the shadows and show the world that this underdog was more than a mere afterthought in the race for greatness.

A Start Full of Surprises

The start of the Kentucky Derby is an exhilarating spectacle — filled with energy, anticipation, and the undeniable tension of a race that can change a horse's life in a matter of minutes. As the horses lined up in their starting gates, the atmosphere was electric, but for Sovereignty, the drama was just beginning. Despite being given long odds and overlooked by nearly every major pundit and bettor, he stood as an enigma in a field full of favorites. The bell rang, the gates burst open, and a thrilling start unfolded that no one, least of all the public, could have predicted.

From the very first moment of the race, the energy was palpable. The horses shot forward, with the favorites quickly taking the early lead, as expected. The media had long focused on the top contenders, and the betting world was waiting for the big names to make their mark. Sovereignty, however, began to make his move in a way that surprised everyone. His start was smooth, unhurried, but unmistakably strong. As the pack surged forward, he began to find his rhythm, settling into a steady, powerful stride that kept him in the mix without overexerting himself.

What made Sovereignty's start even more remarkable was the way he handled the chaos around him. The Derby is notorious for being one of the most competitive and unpredictable races, and with so many horses jostling for position, it can be easy for a less experienced horse to become flustered. But not Sovereignty. He remained calm, focused, and consistent. While the favorite horses jockeyed for the lead, Sovereignty quietly worked his way through the pack, moving up with strategic precision. His jockey, equally calm and focused, steered him with subtle but effective cues, guiding him forward without rushing.

As the race continued, it was clear that Sovereignty was no longer just a participant—he was becoming a true contender. His progress was steady, his movements deliberate, and as the field began to thin out, it was clear that he wasn't fading. In fact, Sovereignty was just getting started. The early predictions had underestimated him, and with each passing furlong, his position improved. His steady, unspectacular approach began to stand in stark contrast to the erratic rush of the other horses, who were beginning to tire or falter.

When the pack reached the final stretch, Sovereignty was still in the hunt. The favorites had lost some of their shine, and Sovereignty—unlike many others—had plenty of fight left. The world was watching now, and the surprise wasn't just that he was still in the race, but that he was pushing ahead, closing in on the leaders with a powerful burst of speed.

Sovereignty's start, though quiet and unassuming, had been a start full of surprises. With each stride, he proved that his victory wouldn't be decided by pedigree, odds, or public opinion—it would be decided by heart, determination, and the quiet belief that he had something more to give. What began as a modest entrance into the race soon became a story of redemption, as Sovereignty, against all expectations, positioned himself for a finish that would redefine the Derby and reshape the future of racing.

Weathering the Pressure

As the Kentucky Derby unfolded and Sovereignty continued to charge ahead, the pressure intensified—not just from the competition, but from the weight of expectations, both public and internal. The Derby is not just a race; it's a test of nerves, focus, and resilience. In the midst of the roar of the crowd, the chaos of the track, and the immense pressure of the occasion, Sovereignty remained an embodiment of composure and focus. While other horses might have faltered under the immense weight of the moment, Sovereignty seemed to thrive under pressure, handling the tumult around him with an uncanny calmness that belied his underdog status.

The first signs of Sovereignty's mental toughness began to emerge as the horses thundered down the stretch. With each passing second, the pressure mounted. The favorites surged ahead, the crowd screamed, and the jockeys gave everything they had to guide their horses. Yet Sovereignty didn't rush. He didn't panic or try to match the early speed of the front runners. He stayed in his rhythm, a quiet force of nature, steadily closing the gap between himself and the leaders. His jockey, experienced and calm, knew that this was the critical moment—not just physically, but mentally. He needed to guide Sovereignty through the pressure without overwhelming him. They trusted each other, and it was that bond that allowed them both to keep their heads amid the frenzy.

It wasn't just the other horses that Sovereignty had to contend with. The weight of public opinion—fueled by his 50-1 odds—lingered as an invisible burden. Everyone had written him off. The press had barely acknowledged him, the betting world had dismissed him, and even in the paddock, he was seen as an outsider.

But Sovereignty never carried that weight on his shoulders. Where many would have let the noise of the crowd and the expectations of the world distract them, Sovereignty remained steadfast in his pursuit. His mind was sharp, focused only on the task at hand, and he was determined not to let the moment overwhelm him.

As they approached the final furlong, Sovereignty began to show his true power. The field had been thinned, and what had once been a chaotic pack of horses now resembled a race for glory. It was here, in the final stretch, that the pressure could either make or break a horse. Some horses faltered, their energy spent too soon, while others showed signs of exhaustion. But Sovereignty surged. He wasn't the fastest out of the gate, nor did he lead the pack at the start, but when it mattered most, when every heartbeat and every breath counted, he found a reserve of energy that pushed him forward.

The pressure of the Kentucky Derby was a storm that others would succumb to, but Sovereignty weathered it. His ability to stay calm under such intense circumstances—both in terms of physical exertion and psychological pressure—was what set him apart. He wasn't just racing against the other horses; he was racing against doubt, against the odds, and against expectations. And as he crossed the finish line, it wasn't just the race that had been won; it was the ultimate test of his character. Sovereignty had proven that mental fortitude, combined with raw talent, could overcome even the most intense pressure. His victory wasn't just a triumph of speed—it was a triumph of composure, resilience, and heart.

Chapter 7
The Race That Rewrote History

The 2025 Kentucky Derby was shaping up to be one of the most thrilling and unpredictable in recent memory. As the gates sprang open and the horses surged forward, the history of the race was being rewritten—though no one knew it yet. Sovereignty, the horse who had been written off by the press, dismissed by the sponsors, and ignored by the betting world, was already proving the world wrong. The other contenders, the media darlings with pedigrees and records of triumph, had launched into their typical fast starts, but Sovereignty wasn't concerned with their reputations or the spotlight that had been cast upon them. His race, in this moment, was his own.

As the field bolted out of the starting gates, the first furlongs of the race were always going to be crucial. The early stages of the Derby are often a test of speed and positioning, with the horses jostling for position in the first few moments. Sovereignty, with his quiet yet powerful stride, began the race calmly, not pushing too hard to stay with the leaders but maintaining a steady, confident pace. His start was smooth, steady, and unhurried—a stark contrast to the chaos unfolding around him. While the frontrunners surged ahead, battling for the early lead, Sovereignty didn't get caught up in the frantic pace. His jockey, with unshakable focus, allowed him to find his rhythm. It was a calculated approach, one that showed wisdom and patience. The pace of the leaders was frantic, but Sovereignty knew his race wasn't won in the first few furlongs. His training, which had focused so heavily on endurance, was about to shine. Sovereignty, unhurried and calm, nestled in among the pack, letting the leaders pull away as he conserved his energy for the battles that would come later. The field was filled with expectation, with every eye on the favorites, but Sovereignty's calmness stood out. While the favorite horses jockeyed for the lead, Sovereignty quietly worked his way through the pack, moving up with strategic precision. His jockey, equally calm and focused, steered him with subtle but effective cues, guiding him forward without rushing.

As the horses neared the final stretch, it became clear that this wasn't going to be another typical Derby. The favorites, worn out from the early sprint, began to show signs of fatigue. The race had taken its toll, and the field had started to thin out. The real contenders were emerging, and Sovereignty was one of them. By this point in the race, the stakes were higher than ever. The pack was still bunched together, but it was evident that Sovereignty was in prime position to make a move. His jockey, knowing exactly when to ask for more, began to encourage the colt to pick up the pace. And just as the leaders started to slow, Sovereignty came alive. His steady, calculated approach was now paying off. The gap between him and the frontrunners closed with every stride. It wasn't just his physical strength that propelled him forward—it was his mental toughness. Where others had faltered under the pressure of the race, Sovereignty thrived. His steady, unassuming rise was a testament to the training that had prepared him for this moment. The final stretch, with its roar of the crowd and the pounding of hooves on the turf, was a battle of wills. And Sovereignty's will was as strong as any of the famed colts that had been dominating the sport for years. With each passing stride, he gained ground, edging closer to the frontrunners who had once seemed so untouchable.

As they approached the final furlong, the world watched in disbelief. The favorites had been battling fiercely all race long, but Sovereignty had remained patient, waiting for the perfect moment to strike. And when that moment came, he surged forward with a burst of speed that no one had anticipated. The Derby was a race of legends, a race that had seen its share of iconic moments, but Sovereignty's final push would go down as one of the most dramatic in the history of the sport. With only a few strides left, Sovereignty and his jockey hit their stride, passing the tired leaders. The crowd roared as the underdog surged ahead, his powerful stride carrying him across the finish line. Sovereignty had done the impossible. He had not only won the 2025 Kentucky Derby—he had rewritten the history books. As he crossed the line, it was clear that Sovereignty's victory was more than just a race won—it was a statement. Against all odds, he had defied expectations, proving that heart, determination, and belief could triumph over pedigree and public opinion. In that moment, Sovereignty was no longer just a horse from humble beginnings—he was a champion, an icon, and a symbol of what it truly means to be an underdog.

The Opening Furlongs

The opening furlongs of the Kentucky Derby are often seen as the most crucial moments of the race. In those first few seconds, horses jostle for position, establishing their place within the pack, and setting the tone for the rest of the race. It's a delicate balance—riders must push for speed, but they also have to avoid burning out too quickly, especially when competing against a field of horses with the pedigree and reputation of the Kentucky Derby's usual contenders. In 2025, however, as the gates opened and the horses surged forward, it quickly became clear that the opening furlongs would tell a different story—a story of an underdog defying expectations and turning heads for all the right reasons.

Sovereignty, the horse who had been dismissed by the media, ignored by sponsors, and given long odds by the bookmakers, stood poised at the starting gate. His calmness was palpable, an unassuming yet steady presence among a field of highly celebrated horses. The favorites—those with gleaming records and high-profile owners—broke out of the gate with speed, as expected. They surged ahead with precision and confidence, jockeys expertly positioning them to secure the best ground. But Sovereignty, with his unhurried start, immediately set himself apart from the others. He wasn't trying to keep up with the flashier horses—he was focused, calm, and steady, keeping a measured pace without being caught up in the early frenzy.

The race's early pace was frantic, with several horses vying for the lead. The media's attention was drawn to them, the darlings of the Derby, but Sovereignty wasn't bothered by the attention. He knew his race was a marathon, not a sprint. In the early furlongs, he chose not to engage in the wild battle for the front. Instead, he tucked in comfortably behind the leading group, conserving energy and positioning himself carefully for the long stretch that lay ahead. His jockey, equally calm, guided him with a gentle hand, urging him forward but never pushing him to race beyond his limits.

As the field stretched out and the horses jockeyed for better positions, Sovereignty's progress was steady, measured, and unhurried. He didn't try to rush ahead to chase down the frontrunners, but instead stayed within himself, allowing his natural stride to carry him forward. His movement was fluid, effortless, and deceptively quick. While the favorites burned energy early, Sovereignty seemed to glide, letting the frenetic pace of others leave them behind.

What was most remarkable about the opening furlongs, though, was how Sovereignty handled the noise and the chaos around him. The crowd, the thunder of hooves, the pressure of the race—it all seemed to wash over him without disrupting his focus. The other horses around him had all the flash and attention, but Sovereignty was, in a way, invisible to the external noise. The expectations of the media, the weight of the Derby, and the distractions surrounding him were nothing more than background noise to the determined colt. The calmness of his demeanor in those first few furlongs became more than just a physical trait—it was the foundation of his mental resilience.

As the pack began to stretch out over the first half mile, Sovereignty's position in the field began to reveal itself. He wasn't a contender for the lead at that point, but he was far from falling behind. With each stride, he moved steadily through the pack, keeping up with the pace but not expending too much energy. The favorites, racing ahead, took the early advantage, but Sovereignty's quiet, consistent run had placed him in a favorable spot without the exhaustion others were already starting to show.

The early stages of the Derby often set the tone for the rest of the race. In most cases, the horses that lead early maintain their positions and fight for the front in the final furlongs. However, Sovereignty was proving that the race was far from decided. In fact, it was only just beginning. As he moved with calm precision through the opening furlongs, it became clear that Sovereignty's approach was far different from the others—he wasn't here to race against the other horses in the traditional sense. Instead, he was pacing himself, waiting for the moment when his heart, his resilience, and his patience would turn the race in his favor.

The opening furlongs were just the beginning of a race that would defy expectations and rewrite history. While other horses rushed to establish dominance, Sovereignty showed the true power of quiet determination. He had no flashy start, no media buzz, no high-profile fanfare. But as the race unfolded, Sovereignty's steady, focused approach was slowly proving to be exactly what he needed to not just finish the race—but to make his mark as a true contender. And in the end, it wasn't just about the quick start—it was about the patience to stay the course and let the race unfold on his own terms.

The Final Stretch

As the Kentucky Derby neared its final stretch, the atmosphere in Churchill Downs was electric. The crowd, once filled with eager speculation and anticipation, now simmered with tension as the race's outcome began to take shape. The leaders, those horses who had surged ahead in the early stages of the race, were beginning to show signs of exhaustion. The gap between the frontrunners and the rest of the field had narrowed, and the real battle for the finish line was about to begin. It was in this moment, when the race seemed destined to follow the script of favorites dominating the final stretch, that Sovereignty's true power came to the forefront.

Sovereignty, who had quietly nestled in the middle of the pack for most of the race, began to make his move. His early conservatism had set the stage for the final phase of the race—a time when stamina, determination, and a deep reservoir of energy were crucial. While others had burned through their reserves in the frantic opening furlongs, Sovereignty's steady, measured pace had allowed him to remain fresh. The true test of a racehorse's endurance comes not in the early stages, but in the final stretch, and this was where Sovereignty would shine.

As Sovereignty surged forward, it was clear that he wasn't just racing against the other horses—he was racing against time, against the public perception that had already written him off as an underdog, and against the overwhelming pressure of the moment. He wasn't just an entry in the Derby anymore—he was a force to be reckoned with. The leaders, who had dominated the race up to this point, were now being overtaken by the determined colt who had stayed just behind, waiting for the right moment to strike. The jockey, with calm confidence, guided Sovereignty through the final stretch, urging him on with precision rather than aggression. There was no frantic pushing or wild maneuvering. This was a controlled, deliberate surge toward the finish line, each stride echoing the months of preparation that had led to this one defining moment.

What made Sovereignty's final push so remarkable was the way he seemed to glide past his competitors. The front-runners, many of them exhausted from the grueling pace, were beginning to slow. The pressure of the Derby, the weight of expectations, had taken its toll. But Sovereignty, with his steady rhythm and unwavering focus, showed no signs of tiring. His muscles, finely tuned from months of training, seemed to propel him forward with increasing intensity, while the leaders struggled to maintain their pace. The gap between

Sovereignty and the front-runners shrank with every stride, his raw power and stamina pushing him ahead.

With the finish line in sight, the crowd's excitement reached a fever pitch. The roar of the crowd seemed to surge with every passing second as Sovereignty, once the underdog, moved into contention for the lead. The favorites, now fading, were desperately trying to hold their positions, but it was clear that Sovereignty had the momentum on his side. His legs, strong and steady, were eating up the track, closing in on the finish line with unmatched determination. The Derby, once a race that seemed destined for the familiar names, was now Sovereignty's to take. It was an improbable surge, a moment of pure athleticism that no one had predicted.

As Sovereignty closed the gap, the tension in the air was almost unbearable. The announcer's voice rang out, building excitement as the horses neared the final yards. For Sovereignty's team, there was no longer any doubt. The race had shifted. His moment had arrived. With a final, powerful burst, Sovereignty surged ahead, his stride lengthening with perfect timing, as if he had been waiting for this exact moment to reveal his true power.

The final stretch was a battle of strength, stamina, and resolve. The other horses had given everything they had, but Sovereignty's steady and patient approach had given him the advantage. He had been underestimated from the start, but now, in the final moments of the race, it was clear that he was not only a contender—he was a champion. Sovereignty crossed the finish line, first, in an astounding display of perseverance, proving to the world that he had not only earned his place in the Derby, but that he had come to dominate it. The crowd erupted in disbelief and admiration, as the underdog story of the century unfolded before their eyes.

The final stretch of the 2025 Kentucky Derby had been a thrilling and unexpected ride, one that would go down in history as a testament to the power of patience, endurance, and belief. Sovereignty had proven, in the most dramatic way possible, that true champions are made not just by pedigree, but by the heart, determination, and quiet strength that can push through when the odds are against them. And in that final stretch, Sovereignty did not just cross the finish line—he rewrote the history of the Kentucky Derby, forever cementing his legacy as one of its most unforgettable champions.

Crossing the Line

As Sovereignty approached the final yards of the 2025 Kentucky Derby, every eye in Churchill Downs was fixed on him. He had started the race as an outsider—underdog, overlooked, and dismissed by both the media and the betting world. Yet here he was, surging forward with the power and precision of a seasoned champion. The crowd was on the edge of their seats, the deafening roar building with every stride, as Sovereignty's moment had finally arrived.

With each passing second, the favorites began to falter, their earlier burst of speed beginning to wane under the relentless pressure of the race. The Derby, as it always does, was proving to be a true test of stamina, resilience, and mental fortitude. For the horses who had spent themselves in the opening furlongs, this was the moment when their earlier bursts would either carry them across the finish line or betray them. But Sovereignty, who had quietly bided his time, was not one of them. He had paced himself with discipline and patience, conserving his energy while others had rushed ahead.

And now, as the field thinned out, his well-timed surge into contention made it clear that he had been holding something special in reserve.

Sovereignty's jockey, with a steady hand and sharp instincts, guided the colt with precision. As the finish line loomed closer, the tension reached a fever pitch. It was clear that the race was no longer about just completing the track—it was about seizing an opportunity that few had thought possible. The leaders, once confident and commanding, were visibly weakening, their strides shortening as fatigue began to set in. Sovereignty, on the other hand, had found his rhythm, and his final push was not only impressive—it was inevitable.

With the finish line drawing closer, Sovereignty's chestnut coat gleamed in the sunlight, his powerful legs eating up the ground beneath him. The gap between him and the frontrunners, which had once seemed insurmountable, continued to close. The final stretch of the race felt like a moment of destiny for Sovereignty. As the other horses struggled to maintain their speed, he seemed to glide over the turf, propelled forward by a combination of strength, heart, and unwavering belief.

The crowd, which had once been divided by expectations and predictions, now stood in collective awe. The roar of the thousands of spectators grew louder, swelling with the excitement of the underdog story unfolding before their eyes. The race that had seemed predetermined was now an open competition, and Sovereignty was showing the world what it meant to defy the odds. His stride became more powerful, more confident, as he closed in on the finish line. With each passing second, the unthinkable was becoming a reality—Sovereignty, the horse no one had expected to challenge, was now in a position to win.

In those final moments, it was as if time had slowed down. The cheers from the crowd echoed through the air, but Sovereignty remained focused, his mind sharp and clear as he closed in on the line. His jockey, never wavering, urged him forward with quiet confidence, knowing that this was the moment when all the hard work, the sacrifices, and the belief would pay off. Sovereignty was racing not just for victory, but for redemption—a horse who had been underestimated from the start, now on the verge of rewriting history.

The final few strides were a blur of speed, energy, and pure willpower. The crowd stood, silent for a split second, before erupting into a deafening roar as Sovereignty crossed the finish line. It was official: the underdog had won the 2025 Kentucky Derby. Sovereignty, against all odds, had defied every expectation, every obstacle, and every prediction to claim the most prestigious race in the world.

As the jockey raised his whip in triumph, the realization of what had just happened began to settle in. Sovereignty's victory wasn't just a win—it was a statement. It was a victory for the overlooked, for those who are written off before they even have a chance. Sovereignty had proven that heart, grit, and determination could overcome even the most impossible odds.

In the blink of an eye, the Derby was transformed from a race about pedigree and power into a celebration of perseverance and belief. Sovereignty's victory was a reminder that champions aren't always the ones who are picked to win—they are the ones who refuse to accept defeat. As Sovereignty's team celebrated the extraordinary victory, they knew they had just witnessed a moment that would go down in history, a moment that would be remembered for years to come. Sovereignty had not only crossed the finish line—he had forever secured his place as a legend of the sport, proving that sometimes, the most remarkable victories come from the most unexpected places.

Chapter 8
After the Finish Line

The race was over, but the story of Sovereignty's victory had only just begun. As the colt crossed the finish line in a breathtaking surge of power and determination, the crowd at Churchill Downs erupted into a deafening roar, a sound that seemed to reverberate through the very ground beneath their feet. For the thousands of spectators who had gathered, many of whom had placed their faith in the more glamorous favorites, Sovereignty's victory was not just an upset—it was a moment of pure, unadulterated magic. The energy in the air was electric, a mixture of disbelief and elation. In an instant, Sovereignty had become a living legend.

But as the roar of the crowd began to fade, the impact of the victory rippled through the racing world and beyond. Media outlets, who had long ignored Sovereignty and dismissed his chances, suddenly found themselves scrambling to report on the most unexpected winner in Kentucky Derby history. The news spread like wildfire, with headlines declaring Sovereignty's win a historic triumph for the underdog. Journalists, whose earlier coverage had failed to even mention his name, were now writing glowing reports about the horse that had stunned the racing world. Experts who had predicted his defeat were forced to reckon with the reality of his strength, resilience, and determination. Sovereignty wasn't just a horse who won a race; he was a symbol of everything that was possible when the odds were stacked against you and you refused to back down.

In the aftermath of the race, the shockwaves were felt not just in the horse racing community, but across various industries. Sponsorship deals that had been previously denied to Sovereignty's team were now on the table, as brands rushed to align themselves with the colt who had defied the world's expectations. The Derby had always been more than just a race—it was a global event, and Sovereignty's victory had captured the imaginations of people far beyond the realm of racing fans. From casual observers to industry professionals, Sovereignty's win had become the talk of the town. In a world where success is often measured by pedigree and connections, Sovereignty had shown that with the right heart and the right people behind you, anything was possible.

As the world took a collective breath, Sovereignty's name began to echo in places it had never been heard before. What was once a horse overlooked by the press, ignored by sponsors, and dismissed by the public had now become a household name. The media, who had failed to see his potential, now made him the centerpiece of their coverage, drawing attention not just to his win but to the remarkable story behind it. Sovereignty's victory became more than just a Derby win—it became a narrative of resilience, a triumph of belief over skepticism, and a testament to the fact that sometimes, the greatest victories come from the most unexpected places. The roar of the crowd, the shockwaves in the media, and the growing recognition of his name would forever mark the moment that Sovereignty transformed from a mere contender into a living legend, whose story would be told for generations to come.

The Roar of the Crowd

The moment Sovereignty crossed the finish line, a deafening roar erupted from the crowd at Churchill Downs. It was a sound like no other—a primal, jubilant, and utterly electrifying expression of disbelief and elation. For those who had been standing in the stands, watching the race unfold with the knowledge that the favorites were in the lead, the sudden surge of the unassuming underdog was nothing short of astonishing. Sovereignty, once written off and overlooked, had just surged past every expectation and claimed the most prestigious race in the world, and the crowd's response was immediate and overwhelming. The roar that filled the air was not just a cheer for a horse crossing the line; it was a resounding affirmation of the impossible, a victory of resilience and hope over predictability and pedigree.

The reaction was immediate—a wave of emotion that rippled through the crowd and spread from one section of the grandstands to the next. In an instant, the atmosphere shifted from nervous anticipation to ecstatic celebration. The kind of energy that only the Kentucky Derby can create surged through the air, as thousands of voices cried out in unison, embracing the thrilling, unexpected result. Many of those gathered had placed their bets on the horses who had been hyped up by the media, the ones with the glossy pedigrees, the heavy favorite contenders, and yet none of those favorites had claimed victory. Sovereignty, the horse no one thought could win, was now the star of the day.

Sovereignty's victory wasn't just a win for his team—it was a moment that broke the mold of what people expected from the Derby. The public had been conditioned to think that success in the race was synonymous with pedigree, celebrity status, and extensive media coverage. But Sovereignty's triumph was different. His victory wasn't about fitting into the traditional narrative—it was about breaking free from the preconceived notions that surrounded him. For the crowd, the roar wasn't just a cheer for an underdog winning; it was a celebration of everything that could be achieved when you believed in the impossible.

The overwhelming noise wasn't confined to the stands alone. The roar reverberated throughout the entire venue, through the paddocks, the barns, and even the backstretch. It was a sound that transcended the physical space of the racetrack and became a symbolic manifestation of the moment. People in the crowd had witnessed something truly special—a race that would be remembered for years to come, not because of the pedigreed horses that had been expected to dominate, but because of the underdog, the long shot, who defied all odds and took his place in history.

Sovereignty's name echoed through the track, carried by the wind, as his victory became a collective experience that united fans, bettors, and casual observers alike. Strangers high-fived, hugged, and celebrated together, sharing in the pure, unfiltered joy of witnessing something truly remarkable. It was a moment that transcended mere competition—this was a celebration of defiance, of heart, and of the power of hard work overcoming expectations. The sound of the crowd wasn't just about the victory on the track—it was the sound of a dream coming true. For Sovereignty's connections—his owner, trainer, jockey, and the small, dedicated team that had worked tirelessly behind the scenes—it was the culmination of years of sacrifice, belief, and commitment.

In the grandstands, the media buzzed with excitement. Journalists, whose earlier predictions had written Sovereignty off as a non-factor in the race, now scrambled to rewrite their narratives. Interviews, commentaries, and reports filled the airwaves, but none could capture the raw, emotional power of what had just happened. The roar of the crowd was more than just a loud sound; it was a symbol of the collective shock and awe that had taken hold of the entire venue. It was the sound of an industry being forced to rethink its assumptions, to recognize that sometimes, it isn't pedigree or fame that produces greatness—it's heart, grit, and the willingness to fight for an impossible dream.

For those who had been there to witness Sovereignty's improbable rise to victory, the roar of the crowd would forever remain etched in their memory. It was a sound that encapsulated the essence of the Kentucky Derby itself—unpredictable, exhilarating, and a celebration of the human spirit. Sovereignty's win wasn't just about the horse; it was about every person who had ever been overlooked, underestimated, or written off. The crowd's roar was a resounding declaration: sometimes the greatest victories come from those who are least expected, and those victories are the ones that leave a lasting impact on the sport, the fans, and the history of the Kentucky Derby.

Media Reactions and Shockwaves

In the world of horse racing, media coverage is often as important as the race itself. Journalists, broadcasters, and industry experts alike build the narrative before the horses even step onto the track. The Kentucky Derby, in particular, is a spectacle that draws global attention, with pre-race coverage often defining who the public believes are the real contenders. Sovereignty, the horse dismissed by so many, was an afterthought in the eyes of the press.

He had been largely ignored in the weeks leading up to the race, with media outlets focusing their attention on the usual favorites—those horses with illustrious bloodlines, storied histories, and high-profile trainers. But when Sovereignty crossed the finish line first in one of the most stunning upsets in Derby history, the shockwaves reverberated throughout the media world.

Journalists who had spent weeks hyping up the expected frontrunners now found themselves scrambling to rewrite their pre-race coverage. Sovereignty's victory left the media scrambling for words, as their expectations had been shattered in real-time. The narrative that had been so carefully crafted—of the elite horses vying for the crown—suddenly felt irrelevant. Sovereignty had not only upset the favorites, but had done so with a quiet, composed determination that no one had anticipated. The media was forced to reckon with the magnitude of the moment. Sovereignty wasn't just another horse crossing the finish line—he had changed the game, and the press had to catch up.

Television stations and print media outlets alike pivoted quickly. The major sports networks, which had been focused on tracking the movements of the other high-profile contenders, shifted their coverage to center on Sovereignty. The headlines began to change, reflecting a new narrative: "Sovereignty Stuns the World" and "The Underdog Who Did the Impossible." Analysts and racing experts, who had earlier dismissed him as a long shot, were now eating their words. Interviews with trainers, owners, and jockeys were re-scripted, as they spoke about how they had always believed in Sovereignty's potential. They recounted the underdog story of his rise from obscurity, and suddenly, the same qualities that had been overlooked became the story of the hour: resilience, heart, and the ability to prove the world wrong.

Across social media, the reaction was equally intense. Sovereignty's name became a trending topic within moments of the victory. Fans who had placed their bets on the favorites now found themselves caught in the whirlwind of excitement surrounding the colt's unexpected success. Racing forums, once focused on the familiar stars, shifted gears. Conversations turned from analyzing bloodlines to celebrating a horse who, against all odds, had not just won the Derby but had done so with such grace and poise.

But perhaps the most significant media reaction came from the sponsors and advertising companies who had turned their backs on Sovereignty in the lead-up to the race. Those who had once dismissed him as a non-starter now found themselves scrambling to capitalize on the colt's newfound fame. Major corporate sponsors, who had previously thrown their weight behind horses with more visible pedigrees, began to offer Sovereignty's team lucrative endorsement deals. Brands that had ignored him during the lead-up to the Derby now realized they had missed an opportunity to align with an unlikely champion. The shockwaves of his victory were felt beyond the racetrack, reaching the marketing world, where fortunes are made based on public perception. Sovereignty had not only won a race; he had shifted the entire dynamic of how success in horse racing was viewed in the media.

The story of Sovereignty's victory wasn't just about a horse winning against the odds; it was a powerful reminder to the media that sometimes the most captivating narratives don't fit into neatly constructed boxes. The press had been so focused on the known quantities that they failed to see the potential in the underdog. Sovereignty, with his calm demeanor and unwavering determination, had shown them that anything is possible. The shockwaves created by his victory rippled outwards, forcing the industry and its media arm to rethink their assumptions about racehorses, success, and what makes a champion.

In the weeks and months that followed, Sovereignty's victory continued to dominate the headlines. His name became synonymous with the kind of underdog success story that resonates far beyond the world of horse racing. Journalists who had once dismissed him now found themselves revisiting their coverage of the race, rethinking their assumptions about what it takes to win at the highest level. Sovereignty's victory wasn't just about beating the odds on the track—it was a reminder that, in sports and in life, sometimes the greatest victories come from those who are most often overlooked. The media had learned a lesson: the best stories are not always the ones that fit into a predictable script, but rather the ones that defy expectations and rewrite history in the process.

Sovereignty's Name Echoes

As Sovereignty crossed the finish line, an unexpected champion in the 2025 Kentucky Derby, his name began to echo far beyond the racetrack. The roar of the crowd had barely subsided when the ripple effects of his victory began to spread throughout the media, racing community, and the public consciousness. In an instant, Sovereignty went from being the overlooked underdog to a household name, a symbol of resilience, defiance, and heart. His win wasn't just a triumph in the world of horse racing—it was a story that captured the imagination of millions. As the story of Sovereignty's victory was told and retold, his name became synonymous with the power of persistence and the ability to break through barriers that once seemed insurmountable.

In the days and weeks following the race, Sovereignty's name continued to resonate with people from all walks of life. For fans of horse racing, his victory was a moment to be celebrated and analyzed. His rise from an overlooked competitor to the winner of the most prestigious race in the world turned into a narrative that transcended the sport. Television networks, sports websites, and social media platforms were flooded with coverage of Sovereignty's triumph. Journalists and commentators who had once written him off were now reflecting on the lessons of his victory—lessons about hard work, dedication, and the unpredictability of sports. Interviews with his owner, trainer, and jockey became some of the most watched segments on sports networks. Everyone wanted to know how Sovereignty, the horse no one had believed in, managed to achieve what seemed impossible.

In the world of horse racing, where pedigree, sponsorships, and past performance often determine the level of attention a horse receives, Sovereignty's victory was a disruptive force. The racing world had always focused on the stars—the horses with famous bloodlines, the ones backed by million-dollar investments, and the ones whose performances were consistently in the spotlight. But Sovereignty's victory sent a shockwave through the industry, reminding everyone that greatness doesn't always come with a pedigree or a glossy backstory. Sovereignty's triumph echoed across the racetrack, forcing trainers, owners, and industry experts to reconsider what it means to be a contender. His name became a beacon of hope for every small stable, every underfunded team, and every horse who had been told they didn't belong.

Beyond the confines of the racetrack, Sovereignty's story resonated with people outside the horse racing world. His victory was a reminder of the power of underdogs in every aspect of life. In an age when success is often tied to pedigree, privilege, and fame, Sovereignty became a symbol for anyone who has ever been overlooked or underestimated. His name echoed through social media platforms, where fans shared memes, stories, and tributes to the horse who had defied the odds. The hashtag #SovereigntyShines became a rallying cry for those who felt like outsiders in their own lives. For many, Sovereignty's victory wasn't just about horse racing—it was about belief in the impossible.

Sovereignty's name didn't just echo in the media or among fans. It also reverberated through the world of sponsorships and endorsements. Before the Derby, Sovereignty had been largely ignored by major corporate sponsors, who had instead thrown their weight behind more popular, well-known horses. But in the wake of his stunning victory, the corporate world began to take notice. Brands that had previously overlooked him now saw the immense value in associating their names with the horse who had taken the world by storm. As his fame grew, Sovereignty's owner and trainer were inundated with offers from companies eager to align themselves with the newfound star. From advertisements to merchandise, Sovereignty's name became a powerful marketing tool—a symbol not just of success, but of overcoming adversity.

The shockwaves of Sovereignty's victory also rippled across the international stage. While the Kentucky Derby is a staple of American culture, the race is followed by horse racing enthusiasts around the world. Sovereignty's victory quickly became global news, with racing fans from Europe, Asia, and beyond celebrating the underdog's success. His name was soon mentioned in the same breath as some of the most famous Derby winners in history. In the world of international racing, where the focus is often on established champions, Sovereignty's name carried with it a new kind of recognition—one that broke down barriers and proved that success could come from the most unexpected sources.

In the years to come, Sovereignty's victory would remain a defining moment in Kentucky Derby history. His name would be immortalized in racing lore, inspiring future generations of horse lovers, trainers, and owners to believe in the power of persistence and heart. Sovereignty was no longer just a name on a list of past Derby winners—he was a symbol of everything that makes the sport so captivating: the unpredictability, the drama, and the unforgettable moments that only a race like the Kentucky Derby can provide.

As the world continued to celebrate Sovereignty's incredible triumph, one thing was certain: his name had become more than just a story about a horse who won a race. It had become a symbol of hope, resilience, and the power of believing that anything is possible, no matter the odds. And in the hearts and minds of those who had witnessed his victory, Sovereignty's name would echo forever.

Chapter 9
Redefining the Underdog

Sovereignty's victory in the 2025 Kentucky Derby was not just an extraordinary achievement for the horse and his team; it was a monumental shift in how we view the concept of the "underdog." In sports, the term "underdog" often carries connotations of improbability, of being outmatched, and of fighting against the odds. For centuries, these underdog stories have captured the hearts of fans, from the underdog athlete to the overlooked team. But Sovereignty's triumph, against all expectations and against the polished pedigrees of the Derby's favorites, redefined what it truly means to be an underdog. His win was more than a surprise—it was a statement that success doesn't come from pedigree or privilege, but from perseverance, heart, and the refusal to accept limitations.

Before the race, Sovereignty was largely ignored by the media, dismissed by analysts, and overlooked by sponsors. He didn't come from a long line of famous racehorses, nor did he have a high-profile owner or trainer. His bloodlines were modest, his history filled with struggles rather than spectacular wins. The world had written him off before he even had a chance to show what he was capable of. But Sovereignty didn't follow the script that had been written for him. Instead, he bucked the trend, defied the expectations, and proved that the term "underdog" was not about weakness—it was about strength, grit, and determination.

Sovereignty's victory challenged the conventional wisdom that a champion's worth is determined by their breeding or their financial backing. It wasn't about who had the most money to spend or the most fame to leverage. It was about the inner strength that drives a horse to keep going, even when the odds are stacked against them. Sovereignty's performance reminded us that being an underdog doesn't mean being doomed to fail—it means finding a way to succeed despite the challenges, to rise above the limitations imposed upon you, and to fight for your place in history. This shift in perspective on what it means to be an underdog extended far beyond the racetrack. Sovereignty's story resonated with anyone who had ever been underestimated, anyone who had been told they couldn't succeed, anyone who had to fight harder to prove their worth. His victory became a beacon for all those who had been counted out, showing them that there is more to success than what the world sees at first glance.

In the wake of his victory, Sovereignty was celebrated not just for his remarkable athleticism, but for the way he embodied the true essence of being an underdog. His victory spoke to the courage that often lies dormant in those who are overlooked and underestimated. It reminded the world that sometimes, the most powerful forces in the world are the ones that aren't immediately visible, the ones that are waiting patiently, steadily preparing for the right moment to prove their worth. Sovereignty's story became the ultimate example of how an underdog can redefine the rules of success, proving that determination, resilience, and heart are often more important than pedigree, wealth, or fame. His name will forever be associated with the idea that, sometimes, the most remarkable victories come from the least expected places.

What Makes an Underdog?

An underdog is often defined by the perception of being at a disadvantage. In sports, business, and life, the underdog is the competitor who faces overwhelming odds, whether due to lack of experience, resources, or recognition. They are the ones who, in the eyes of many, are expected to fail. Yet, it is this very perception of disadvantage that often drives them to greatness. Being an underdog is not simply about being the lowest-ranked contender or the one with the smallest chance of success. It is a mindset—a determination to rise above expectations and prove that success is not always about pedigree, privilege, or preparation. An underdog is someone who is underestimated, but often, it is this underestimation that fuels their desire to succeed.

Sovereignty, in the 2025 Kentucky Derby, was the embodiment of the underdog spirit. His story was one of quiet strength, perseverance, and the drive to overcome the odds. Before the race, no one believed he had a chance. He didn't have the prestigious bloodlines of the other contenders, nor did he have the flashy profile that media outlets gravitated toward. His early career had been modest, and the bookmakers had written him off, offering him 50-1 odds. To the public and the media, Sovereignty was nothing more than a participant—he was not a story, he was an afterthought. But as the Derby unfolded, Sovereignty showed the world what it means to be an underdog.

What truly makes an underdog is their ability to defy expectations. Underdogs are not defined by their perceived disadvantages but by how they use those disadvantages as fuel for success. In Sovereignty's case, his lack of pedigree and media attention were not handicaps—they were the very factors that allowed him to remain unbothered by the pressures that often affect the favorites. While the more hyped horses were chasing the spotlight, Sovereignty focused on the race itself. His approach was methodical, patient, and unwavering. He wasn't in the race to prove anything to anyone else; he was in it to prove something to himself.

Underdogs often face the challenge of fighting against not just the competition, but against preconceived notions about their abilities. The world loves to root for the underdog because we see ourselves in them. We know what it feels like to be counted out, to be told we don't belong, to be overlooked in favor of someone with more resources or a more polished resume. Sovereignty was exactly that—an underdog who fought against the perception that pedigree was the only path to greatness. His victory was a testament to the idea that, often, the greatest achievements come from the most unexpected sources.

An underdog's journey is never easy. They have to overcome the external pressures of doubt and skepticism while battling internal doubts that often come with being underestimated. But it is in this struggle, this constant proving of oneself, that underdogs find their strength. Sovereignty, like many underdogs, was forced to face the challenge of navigating a world where being "good enough" wasn't enough. He had to fight for every bit of respect he gained, and this struggle helped him build a resilience that would ultimately define his victory.

Part of what makes an underdog so compelling is their ability to make the impossible seem possible. There is something inherently inspiring about watching someone who has been written off not only succeed but thrive in the face of adversity. Sovereignty's victory in the Derby wasn't just a triumph of athleticism; it was a triumph of willpower, heart, and determination. His name, once barely mentioned in the lead-up to the race, became synonymous with the idea that anything is possible when you refuse to give up, no matter how improbable success may seem.

At its core, being an underdog is about overcoming limitations—whether they be physical, mental, or societal—and proving that success is often about more than just pedigree or resources. It is about finding strength in adversity, determination in the face of doubt, and belief in the face of skepticism. Sovereignty's victory redefined what it means to be an underdog, proving that success doesn't always come from being the best or the most recognized—it comes from having the heart to keep going when the world tells you that you cannot. And it is this spirit, this relentless drive to prove the doubters wrong, that makes the underdog story so universally compelling.

Courage Over Cost

In a world where wealth, resources, and status often dominate narratives of success, courage becomes the quiet yet powerful force that enables individuals, and in this case, horses, to transcend their circumstances. Sovereignty's victory in the 2025 Kentucky Derby serves as a shining example of how courage, determination, and the refusal to bow to limitations can often surpass the advantages that money and prestige offer. His win was not just a testament to his physical capabilities as a horse but a celebration of the courage to persevere against a backdrop of doubt, skepticism, and overwhelming odds.

At the heart of Sovereignty's story was a profound sense of belief—not in the resources that could be thrown behind him, but in the strength of the bond he shared with his trainer, owner, and jockey. From the very beginning of his journey, Sovereignty was not afforded the luxury of being the chosen one, the favorite, or the horse with a high-profile backer. Unlike many of the Derby's front-runners, Sovereignty didn't have the immense financial backing or the famous lineage that typically guarantees attention and sponsorships. His owner didn't have the kind of wealth that could easily buy a champion horse, and his connections in the racing world weren't those that would immediately thrust him into the media spotlight. Yet, what Sovereignty lacked in financial support, he more than made up for in heart and spirit.

In the face of this disparity, Sovereignty's story became one about courage over cost. In horse racing, as in many industries, financial clout is often seen as the key to success. Wealth can buy the best trainers, the most luxurious facilities, and access to the best breeding programs. It can also guarantee media exposure and lucrative sponsorship deals that help elevate a horse's profile. But while these resources can provide a significant advantage, they cannot buy heart, determination, or the will to succeed. Sovereignty was never going to win the Derby by simply relying on the financial resources at his disposal. Instead, it was his courage—his ability to keep fighting when the odds were stacked against him—that ultimately carried him to victory.

Sovereignty's courage manifested in the form of patience, resilience, and mental fortitude. While the more celebrated horses raced ahead early, using their speed and pedigree to create gaps, Sovereignty remained steady. His strength was not in his flashy performance but in his quiet determination. The early part of the race was a test of both physical and mental stamina. It was clear from the start that Sovereignty was not the fastest out of the gate, nor was he leading the pack in the early stages. But what set him apart was his ability to pace himself, to stay calm and composed, and to push forward when others faltered. Sovereignty's courage was found not in rushing ahead but in holding steady, trusting in the strength he had built over months of quiet training.

In the face of enormous competition, with a field filled with horses that had the best bloodlines, the biggest sponsors, and the most media attention, Sovereignty's courage was a quiet but powerful statement. The Derby is often seen as a race of pedigree, a showcase of wealth and influence. Horses with multi-million dollar price tags and famous names in their bloodlines typically dominate the headlines. But Sovereignty's courage—his ability to stay the course and trust in his own abilities—showed that true greatness is not always about what you can buy or who you know. It's about belief, perseverance, and the courage to prove that, sometimes, the heart can outweigh even the deepest pockets.

This courage was not just visible on the track—it was present in every aspect of Sovereignty's journey to the Derby. His team, too, demonstrated the kind of courage that money couldn't buy. They chose to invest in him not because of his pedigree or his public profile but because they believed in his potential. His trainer, who had seen the fire within Sovereignty, dedicated time and effort to nurture his strengths, knowing that this horse, though overlooked, had something extraordinary within him. Sovereignty's owner also saw beyond the financial costs and limitations, choosing instead to invest in the horse's future because of the raw potential they saw in him. These were decisions made on courage—decisions that cost more than just money; they required faith in the unseen, in the belief that Sovereignty's heart and spirit would carry him further than anyone could have predicted.

Sovereignty's victory was a reminder that courage, more than financial resources, can drive success. It's the kind of courage that pushes someone—or something—forward when the path is uncertain, when the doubters are louder than the supporters, and when the world seems stacked against you. Sovereignty, against all expectations, proved that the heart's power is sometimes more valuable than money. His courage to rise above, to stay steady in the face of pressure, and to believe in himself even when the world doubted him, ultimately took him from an outsider to the center of the racing world. Sovereignty's story is one of triumph against the odds, and it serves as a powerful reminder that when courage is prioritized over cost, anything is possible.

A Legend in Hoofbeats

Sovereignty's victory in the 2025 Kentucky Derby didn't just make him a winner—it turned him into a legend. In the world of horse racing, legends are made not by pedigree or money but by moments of extraordinary triumph, the kind that transcends expectations and echoes through history. Sovereignty's story, a tale of underestimation, resilience, and raw courage, would become one of the most celebrated narratives in the sport. His win wasn't just a victory on the racetrack; it was a defining moment that redefined what it meant to be a champion, proving that legends are not always born—they are made through perseverance and heart.

Before the Derby, Sovereignty's name was scarcely mentioned in the same breath as the high-profile contenders. He was considered a long shot, an outsider in a race dominated by horses with illustrious bloodlines and heavy sponsorships. The media had overlooked him, and the betting world had written him off, offering him 50-1 odds. In the world of horse racing, where the spotlight often shines brightest on the pedigreed horses and those with the most financial backing, Sovereignty had none of the advantages. Yet, in the blink of an eye, he defied those odds in a way no one could have predicted.

As the Kentucky Derby unfolded, Sovereignty made his move, slowly but surely, with a quiet determination that made the seasoned favorites look like they were running out of steam. While the media and the crowd fixated on the horses with the big names and the flashy starts, Sovereignty stayed calm, unfazed by the rush of competition around him. His steady pace and resilience began to show in the latter parts of the race, and as the front-runners began to falter, Sovereignty surged ahead with power and precision. What began as a race filled with expectations quickly turned into a story of a horse who had been underestimated every step of the way—until he crossed the finish line in front of the entire world.

The roar of the crowd, the stunned silence of analysts and pundits who had written him off, and the astonished faces of spectators were a testament to the fact that Sovereignty was more than just a Derby winner. He had become a symbol of what it means to defy the odds, to rise above the noise of skepticism, and to embrace the challenge of making history. Sovereignty's victory was a triumph of spirit, a reminder that greatness can come from the most unexpected places, and that sometimes, it's the quiet underdog who ends up rewriting the narrative. In that moment, Sovereignty wasn't just another horse who won a race—he was a legend in the making.

The following weeks and months only added to his legend. Sovereignty's name became synonymous with the idea that persistence, heart, and courage can carry you farther than any financial investment or famous lineage. His story was told and retold in newspapers, on television, and across social media platforms, captivating not just racing enthusiasts but people from all walks of life. He became the face of the underdog story—of someone who, when the world doubted him, believed in himself and emerged victorious. His victory was celebrated not only as a win for horse racing but as a triumph for anyone who had ever been told they couldn't achieve their dreams.

The world's attention shifted toward Sovereignty's team—the trainer, the owner, and the jockey who had always believed in him. The bond they shared with Sovereignty was rooted in trust and faith, a belief in his untapped potential. Unlike the larger teams behind the high-profile horses, Sovereignty's team didn't have vast financial resources or famous connections. What they did have, however, was an unwavering belief in Sovereignty's spirit and ability. Their trust in him became the cornerstone of his success, and together, they had created a champion.

Sovereignty's victory began to reshape perceptions within the racing community. For years, the narrative around the Derby had been that pedigree and sponsorship were the true keys to success. The media had always focused on the horses with the largest investments and the most storied bloodlines. Sovereignty, however, shattered that narrative. His win forced the racing world to acknowledge that greatness cannot always be measured by money or connections—it's about the horse's heart, the strength of the team behind them, and the will to overcome adversity.

Sovereignty's legacy extends beyond his Derby victory. He became a symbol of hope for all those who are overlooked or underestimated. His story proves that being counted out doesn't mean being destined for failure—it means having the opportunity to rise up and show the world that greatness isn't defined by what others think of you, but by what you believe about yourself. His name, which was once nothing more than a whisper in the racing world, now echoes as a reminder that champions are made not just through skill or pedigree but through heart, determination, and the courage to believe when no one else does.

Sovereignty's story would go down as one of the greatest in Kentucky Derby history, not just because of his win but because of how he achieved it. In his hoofbeats, he carried the legacy of every underdog who has ever fought to prove their worth. Sovereignty, the horse no one thought could win, became a legend whose name would be remembered for generations, a symbol of perseverance, courage, and the timeless power of believing in the impossible.

Chapter 10
Legacy in Motion

Sovereignty's victory in the 2025 Kentucky Derby was not just a personal triumph for the horse, his team, and his owner—it marked the beginning of a profound shift in the world of horse racing. His name became synonymous with the essence of what it means to challenge the established order and rewrite the narrative. The Derby, a race long dominated by horses with storied bloodlines, heavy financial backing, and high-profile sponsorships, had just witnessed the rise of an underdog, an unexpected champion, whose victory changed the way the world viewed success in racing.

For years, the narrative surrounding the Kentucky Derby and horse racing, in general, was one of privilege and pedigree. The media, fans, and even the industry itself often placed the greatest importance on a horse's lineage, their financial investment, and the celebrity of their owners. Pedigree was considered a reliable predictor of success, and the horses with the best bloodlines were almost always the ones favored to win. Sovereignty, however, shattered that long-held belief. Without the massive financial backing of wealthy owners or the prestigious bloodlines that the racing world often favored, Sovereignty showed that heart, resilience, and the right team could break through the barriers of wealth and privilege.

In the wake of Sovereignty's incredible performance, a new narrative began to emerge. The underdog story of Sovereignty resonated with fans of all kinds. Those who had never considered horse racing as something accessible to them now found themselves captivated by the colt's journey. Sovereignty's success was a reminder that in a sport often defined by wealth, the most important ingredients for victory were not always money or breeding but belief, persistence, and the courage to defy the odds. His victory not only impacted seasoned racing fans but also drew in a whole new audience that was inspired by his resilience. Sovereignty's story became emblematic of the broader human experience—proving that even the most unlikely contender can rise above expectations and achieve greatness.

This chapter is dedicated to exploring the lasting legacy that Sovereignty has left in the world of horse racing. From changing perceptions of what it means to be a champion to attracting a new generation of fans to the sport, Sovereignty's victory was just the beginning of his impact on the world. His legacy has continued to inspire and challenge the conventional wisdom of the racing industry, and his name is now synonymous with the idea that true champions are often those who are most frequently overlooked. As we look at the impact of Sovereignty's triumph, we will explore how the narrative of racing has shifted, how new fans have found faith in the sport, and where Sovereignty stands today—both in the record books and in the hearts of millions. His journey is far from over, and the legacy he has begun to build is one that will continue to resonate for years to come.

Changing the Narrative in Racing

Sovereignty's victory in the 2025 Kentucky Derby was more than just a personal triumph; it marked a turning point in the way the racing world viewed success. For generations, horse racing had been a sport defined by its emphasis on pedigree, financial backing, and the prominence of owners, trainers, and sponsors. Horses with famous bloodlines, high-priced purchases, and luxurious training stables were often considered the most likely candidates for success. This was the narrative that the sport had adhered to, and it was a narrative that created a clear divide between the "elite" horses and the underdogs. But Sovereignty, the horse who had neither a famous lineage nor the weight of vast sponsorships behind him, upended this age-old narrative in a way that would have lasting implications for the future of the sport.

Before the Derby, Sovereignty was seen as a long shot, a competitor whose chances of winning were considered almost laughable by many in the media and industry. His bloodlines were considered modest at best, and his owner didn't have the financial clout that usually ensures a horse's name is at the front of every headline. The media's focus was on the familiar names, the horses backed by billionaires and high-profile trainers, the horses whose pedigrees were steeped in racing history. Sovereignty, in the eyes of the racing world, was an afterthought. His entry in the Derby was more of a curiosity than a serious contention. The betting odds reflected the world's doubt in his ability to compete—50-1.

Yet, in a single race, Sovereignty shattered the established narrative. His victory not only proved the doubters wrong but also highlighted a glaring truth: the narrative in racing had been overly simplistic, and it had underestimated the power of heart, training, and perseverance. The world watched as Sovereignty surged past horses with superior pedigrees and heavy backing, each stride a defiance of the sport's conventional wisdom. This victory wasn't just a surprise; it was a profound statement that the focus in racing needed to shift. Pedigree, while important, wasn't the only determinant of success. The strength of the individual, the dedication of the team, and the belief in an underdog were just as powerful forces in the pursuit of greatness.

In the days that followed Sovereignty's triumph, the media began to grapple with the implications of his victory. What did it mean for the future of the sport if a horse with little fanfare could outperform the favorites, not just once but on the grandest stage? The old narrative, which placed so much emphasis on wealth, pedigree, and sponsorship, began to be questioned. Racing insiders, who had once valued bloodlines and financial investment above all else, began to recognize that success in horse racing didn't have to be dictated by privilege. Sovereignty's victory proved that a different kind of story could unfold on the racetrack—a story driven by resilience, determination, and belief in the face of doubt.

For many fans of horse racing, Sovereignty's win was a breath of fresh air. It injected new life into a sport that had, in some ways, become predictable. The same names, the same pedigrees, the same wealthy backers—these were the hallmarks of the sport for decades. But Sovereignty's victory reminded everyone that racing was still about more than just the horses and their bloodlines; it was about the passion of the people involved, the effort they put into their horses, and the way they nurtured talent. The race had become about more than just speed—it was a contest of will, and Sovereignty had proven that even the most modest beginnings could lead to extraordinary success.

His triumph also opened up the doors for a broader range of participants to believe that they too could enter the racing world and make their mark, regardless of their background. The idea that wealth and status were prerequisites for success had been a barrier for many aspiring owners and trainers. Sovereignty's win proved that, with the right mindset, dedication, and passion, anyone could rise to the top. His victory was an invitation for future generations of trainers, jockeys, and owners to join the sport, regardless of whether they came from money or had a prestigious name to back them up.

The ripple effect of Sovereignty's victory continued to be felt throughout the racing world. As the story of his win spread, new fans were drawn to the sport. These fans weren't necessarily following the established stars but were captivated by the idea of the underdog—the horse who didn't have everything going for him but still managed to win against the odds. For many, this shift in the narrative was inspiring. It reminded them of the power of perseverance, and how hard work and a belief in oneself can defy even the most entrenched systems.

Sovereignty's victory changed more than just the perceptions of racing fans; it changed the entire framework of the sport itself. He became a symbol for what was possible when the underdog story was given room to breathe, and he proved that racing wasn't just a game for the rich and powerful—it was a sport for anyone with the courage and will to compete. Sovereignty's victory had rewritten the script of the Kentucky Derby and, in doing so, had rewritten the narrative of racing as a whole. The sport would never be the same again, and Sovereignty would forever be remembered as the horse who changed the way we view success in the Derby and beyond.

New Fans, New Faith

Sovereignty's victory in the 2025 Kentucky Derby wasn't just an event for established horse racing fans—it marked a turning point that attracted a whole new generation of fans to the sport. His underdog story, the surprise of his victory, and the sheer joy of seeing a horse overcome all odds resonated with individuals who had never before been invested in the racing world. In a sport traditionally dominated by elitism and a strong focus on pedigree and wealth, Sovereignty's triumph opened the door for new fans from all walks of life, individuals who had been either indifferent or excluded from the sport due to its perceived exclusivity. Sovereignty's win redefined the boundaries of the audience, offering a story that anyone could connect with—whether they were seasoned horse racing enthusiasts or complete newcomers.

Before Sovereignty's victory, the Kentucky Derby, like much of the horse racing world, had often been a spectacle watched by those deeply entrenched in the sport. Media coverage and fan interest typically centered on the famous, well-bred horses with multimillion-dollar backers—the ones with all the resources and spotlight that came with their pedigrees. These horses often captured the hearts of those already familiar with the sport, creating a somewhat insular community of followers. However, Sovereignty's surprising victory disrupted this dynamic. His win was so improbable and filled with elements that almost everyone could root for: the classic underdog against all odds, the fighter with no pedigree but an unshakable spirit. In essence, Sovereignty's victory transcended the barriers of privilege and status that had traditionally defined the sport, reaching out to a broader audience.

The way the media covered Sovereignty's story also played a significant role in drawing new fans to the sport. As soon as Sovereignty crossed the finish line in first place, the story quickly spread across social media, television, and newspapers. Headlines touted the win as one of the greatest underdog stories in recent sports history, and for the first time in many years, the sport of horse racing found itself at the center of a mainstream conversation. Social media platforms buzzed with fans from all over the world sharing memes, videos, and messages of support for Sovereignty, elevating his win beyond the confines of the racetrack and into the cultural mainstream.

These new fans weren't just passive spectators—they were engaged, sharing Sovereignty's story, discussing his journey, and spreading the word about the Kentucky Derby. Sovereignty's victory became a rallying cry for those who had been disillusioned with the mainstream narratives of privilege and financial clout that often dominated the sporting world. Sovereignty represented something more—he symbolized resilience, the belief that even those who come from humble beginnings can make it to the top through hard work and dedication. His story resonated with anyone who had ever felt overlooked, underestimated, or dismissed.

The shift in fan engagement was also reflected in the numbers. The 2025 Kentucky Derby experienced a notable spike in viewership, particularly among younger audiences. While older, traditional fans continued to tune in, it was the younger demographic that had been most captivated by Sovereignty's story. The underdog tale was timeless, but the accessibility and relatability of Sovereignty's journey to victory brought a whole new level of excitement to the sport. Many fans, whether they were casual or first-time viewers, found themselves invested in Sovereignty's journey not because of his bloodline or financial backing, but because of the sheer grit and heart he displayed throughout the race.

The narrative of Sovereignty wasn't just about horse racing—it was a story that transcended the sport itself. It was about fighting against the odds, standing up to the world's expectations, and showing that greatness doesn't always come from wealth or privilege. This universal theme of perseverance and belief in oneself connected with people from all walks of life. His story resonated not only with those familiar with racing but also with people who had never previously considered the sport. Sovereignty gave them something to believe in—an entry point into a world they thought was reserved for the elite. This change in how the sport was perceived was profound, as it injected new energy into a scene that had often been seen as exclusive and out of reach.

In the wake of Sovereignty's victory, his legacy also began to shift the perception of horse racing itself. No longer was the sport solely about pedigree or wealth. It had become a place where heart, perseverance, and the drive to succeed mattered just as much as any monetary investment. The legacy of Sovereignty wasn't just about his win on that day in 2025—it was about how his victory changed the dynamic of the sport, attracting new fans, fostering new faith in the underdog, and inspiring future generations to believe that anything is possible, no matter the odds.

The ripple effects of Sovereignty's win were far-reaching. Horse racing, often seen as a niche sport with a dedicated but limited fanbase, experienced a revival of interest, attracting younger, diverse fans who found in Sovereignty's journey the kind of inspiration they could relate to. These new fans brought energy, enthusiasm, and a sense of inclusivity to the sport—something that had been lacking for years. As Sovereignty's name continued to echo throughout the world, the Kentucky Derby was no longer just an event for the wealthy or the well-connected. It was a celebration of perseverance, determination, and the unexpected, and it became an event that all fans—old and new—could share in.

Where Sovereignty Stands Today

Sovereignty's victory in the 2025 Kentucky Derby remains one of the most remarkable moments in horse racing history, but it is his legacy that continues to impact the sport long after the race ended. Today, Sovereignty stands not only as a champion of the Derby but as a symbol of resilience, the embodiment of an underdog triumphing against the odds. His name has become synonymous with the idea that anything is possible when perseverance, heart, and courage are at the forefront of an endeavor. But where does Sovereignty stand today, beyond the grand stage of the Derby? How has his victory transformed his place in the racing world, and what role does he play in shaping the future of the sport?

In the years since his victory, Sovereignty's name has continued to echo through the horse racing world, though his story has shifted in tone. No longer just an underdog story, Sovereignty's triumph in the Derby redefined what it meant to be a champion. He has since become a symbol for all those who refuse to accept limitations, a testament to the idea that success isn't determined by pedigree or financial backing alone, but by the heart and determination of the individual. Sovereignty's legacy continues to inspire not only horse racing enthusiasts but also anyone who has ever fought to achieve greatness despite the odds.

After the Derby, Sovereignty's profile only grew. His victory, so improbable at the time, made him a household name and drew attention to the sport that had long been reserved for the elite. Racing fans from all walks of life followed Sovereignty's journey with a renewed sense of excitement, watching him race with the kind of respect and admiration typically reserved for more celebrated horses. Sovereignty's story wasn't just about his victory in the Derby—it was about the spirit of competition, the joy of seeing an underdog succeed, and the belief that anything is possible with the right combination of talent, persistence, and heart.

Following his iconic win, Sovereignty became a symbol of hope for aspiring trainers, owners, and jockeys, particularly those who might have felt sidelined by the financial constraints and pedigree-based judgments of the industry. For many, Sovereignty's success was proof that with the right approach, hard work, and dedication, even horses with modest bloodlines and limited resources could rise to greatness. The racing community, once dominated by a few large, wealthy owners and horses with rich pedigrees, began to see the value in giving horses like Sovereignty a chance to shine. His success has influenced how some owners approach their stables, focusing less on the traditional metrics of success and more on the potential of each horse, regardless of their pedigree.

Sovereignty's influence also extended into the commercial side of the sport. Before the Derby, his lack of sponsorship and the absence of media attention had been one of the major obstacles he faced. But after the victory, everything changed. Major brands began to take notice of Sovereignty and his story, realizing the tremendous value in associating their name with a horse whose victory symbolized not just athletic achievement, but a triumph over expectations. Sponsors who had previously overlooked him scrambled to secure endorsement deals, capitalizing on the newfound fame and the emotional connection that Sovereignty had forged with fans around the world.

Today, Sovereignty continues to enjoy a degree of celebrity that many racing champions never experience. He regularly appears at racing events, not just as a competitor but as a living reminder of what is possible in a sport often defined by its elite participants. His success is a point of inspiration for future generations of racing enthusiasts, as they see in Sovereignty the embodiment of what it means to believe in the impossible.

Beyond the racetrack, Sovereignty has played a key role in attracting new fans to the sport of horse racing. His story has been told and retold in documentaries, interviews, and social media campaigns, drawing in a younger, more diverse audience who find themselves inspired by his journey. What was once a niche sport reserved for a select few has found a wider following, thanks in part to Sovereignty's impact. Through his story, the world has come to realize that racing is not just for the wealthy elite, but for anyone who loves the drama, excitement, and beauty of the sport.

While his racing days may eventually come to an end, Sovereignty's impact on horse racing is far from over. His legacy is now embedded in the sport's future, influencing not just the horses who follow him but the people who support and guide them. His story has become a model for what it means to be a champion—not necessarily the fastest, the richest, or the most well-known, but the one who refuses to give up, the one who continues to push forward even when the world doubts them.

Sovereignty's name will continue to stand as a testament to the power of the underdog. His victory wasn't a fluke—it was the culmination of a journey defined by heart, grit, and determination. As he continues to inspire new generations of racing fans, owners, and trainers, Sovereignty remains a legend not just for his Derby win, but for the example he set of what it means to be truly great. In a sport that has long been dominated by the wealthy and the pedigreed, Sovereignty proved that greatness is not always about resources, connections, or history—it's about the will to overcome obstacles and the courage to pursue victory no matter the odds.

Chapter 11
The Road Ahead

Sovereignty's victory in the 2025 Kentucky Derby was not the culmination of his story, but rather the beginning of a new chapter—one that would be shaped by the expectations that followed such a high-profile victory. For many horses, the Derby is the pinnacle of their career, but for Sovereignty, it was a stepping stone to what could be a continued and successful journey in the racing world. The road ahead for a Derby-winning horse is never easy. After achieving such a historic triumph, there is always the pressure to continue to deliver, to live up to the expectations that come with fame and success. But Sovereignty's story, already one of triumph and defiance against the odds, had many more chapters to write.

The challenges Sovereignty faced post-Derby were not just about his physical training and preparation for upcoming races. They were also about managing the newfound attention, the increased stakes, and the added pressure of being seen as a symbol of possibility—proof that even the most unlikely horses could rise to the top. The training for the future would need to be carefully planned, taking into account Sovereignty's past achievements while preparing him for the continued success that was expected of him. The next races, the challenges of maintaining peak performance, and even the delicate matter of his retirement would all play a part in shaping the rest of his legacy.

For a horse who was once overlooked and underestimated, the road ahead was filled with opportunities, but also great challenges. How would Sovereignty handle the pressure of being the reigning Derby champion? Would he continue to perform at such a high level, or would the weight of his victory become a burden? How would his team manage the delicate balance of keeping him competitive while also protecting his future? These were questions that Sovereignty's team would need to answer, as they navigated the next phase of his illustrious career.

One thing was certain: the road ahead was not going to be easy. The training would need to be more strategic than ever before, taking into consideration Sovereignty's unique needs and the expectations that now surrounded him. The upcoming races would come with their own set of challenges, but with each challenge came the potential for greater triumphs, cementing Sovereignty's place in history. As he continued to grow and evolve, the focus would need to be on keeping his spirit and heart intact while preparing him for the demands of the races to come.

This chapter will explore Sovereignty's future—how his team would plan for his continued success, the races that lay ahead, and how they would navigate the complexities of ensuring his legacy as a Derby champion remained intact. The road ahead would be shaped by careful planning, but also by the same qualities that had made Sovereignty a winner: grit, determination, and the heart of an underdog who was never afraid to face the next challenge.

Training for the Future

After Sovereignty's stunning victory in the 2025 Kentucky Derby, his team knew that the future would require as much careful planning and strategy as the journey that had led them to that iconic win. Training for the future wasn't just about physical conditioning; it was about maintaining his mental toughness, managing the increased pressure, and ensuring that he could continue to perform at the highest level without burning out. The goal was to balance his fitness with his well-being, allowing him to continue competing at the top of his game while also setting him up for a potential future in breeding or retirement when the time came.

Sovereignty's training regimen would need to be carefully adjusted to suit his newfound status as a Derby champion. The demands on his body would be greater than ever, as expectations skyrocketed after his victory. The stakes would be higher in every race, and his competitors would be more eager than ever to dethrone the Derby champion. With this in mind, Sovereignty's trainers began to focus on a multi-faceted approach that would not only keep him in peak physical condition but also nurture his resilience and stamina.

First and foremost, Sovereignty's training would need to include careful management of his workload. As a champion, he couldn't afford to be overworked, so the team needed to ensure he was given ample time to rest between races, particularly the more high-profile events. Overtraining could lead to injuries or burnout, something no one wanted for a horse who had already achieved so much. The balance between training and rest became crucial. His trainers took a tailored approach to his workouts, incorporating light and heavy days based on the schedule of upcoming races. For a horse with his unique history and abilities, this would be essential for maintaining peak performance over the long term.

Another critical aspect of training for the future was maintaining Sovereignty's speed and agility, despite the inevitable physical changes that come with age and success. The Derby winner had already proven that he could hold his own against the best, but his trainers were keenly aware that the longer his career lasted, the more focused they would need to be on refining his techniques to preserve his competitive edge. Exercises to improve his acceleration, as well as drills designed to maintain his agility and maneuverability in tight racing conditions, became part of his regular schedule. This would ensure that he was not just maintaining his existing abilities, but also developing new strengths that would help him excel in various race conditions.

Sovereignty's mental state would also play a critical role in his future success. After all, racing isn't just about physical fitness—it's about the horse's mental fortitude and their ability to focus, push through adversity, and perform under pressure. Sovereignty's victory in the Derby had proven that he had the heart of a champion, but his team recognized that maintaining that drive would require careful psychological management. The trainers worked with Sovereignty's handler to make sure that the horse's environment remained calm, positive, and conducive to focus. His daily routines included plenty of social interaction with other horses and time spent outdoors, ensuring he remained mentally sharp and connected to his natural instincts. In addition, Sovereignty's team incorporated varied training environments, from traditional racecourses to quieter, less stressful locations, to help him stay mentally adaptable and avoid becoming too fatigued or anxious about competing.

Given his prominence in the racing world, Sovereignty also became accustomed to media attention, and his trainers knew that handling the pressure of this newfound fame would be just as important as physical preparation. While the media was undoubtedly a tool for promoting the sport, it also came with the potential to distract and overwhelm a racehorse. Sovereignty's team worked hard to keep him out of the spotlight when necessary, giving him space to rest and recover from the demands of fame. They also took great care to protect his routines, ensuring that his focus remained on racing, rather than the noise and pressure that came with being a champion.

The future, however, wasn't just about the upcoming races—it was also about preserving Sovereignty's health for the long term. Racing is demanding, and the impact of a career on a horse's body can be profound. In his training for the future, Sovereignty's team also took proactive steps to manage any signs of strain or discomfort that might arise as he continued to race. Regular veterinary checkups, massage therapy, and monitoring of his joints, muscles, and overall health became regular parts of his routine. This focus on long-term care helped ensure that Sovereignty could remain at the top of his game while also keeping the risk of injury at bay.

Training for the future was about more than just maintaining Sovereignty's speed and endurance. It was about creating a sustainable path for success, ensuring that every step, every race, and every move was part of a carefully crafted strategy to preserve his legacy as a champion while also protecting his well-being. Sovereignty's future was bright, but it would require a thoughtful, balanced approach to ensure he continued to race—and win—at the highest level for as long as possible. Through this meticulous training and care, Sovereignty's team hoped to secure not just future victories but a lasting legacy in the sport of kings.

Next Races and Challenges

After Sovereignty's historic victory in the 2025 Kentucky Derby, the racing world eagerly anticipated what would come next for the young champion. His Derby win had catapulted him to the top of the sport, but with that position came an entirely new set of challenges. The next races on Sovereignty's calendar would be a critical test of his abilities, his resilience, and his capacity to handle the increased pressure of being the reigning Derby champion. Success would not come easily—he would have to prove that his Derby victory was not a fluke and that he was ready to compete at the highest level.

One of the immediate challenges for Sovereignty was maintaining his physical peak. After such a grueling race as the Kentucky Derby, the next races would demand an even higher level of preparation. The trainers and jockeys worked to ensure that Sovereignty's body remained sharp, not just for his next race but for the future events that would follow. The traditional racing calendar included major events such as the Preakness Stakes, the Belmont Stakes, and other key races, each with their own unique demands. Sovereignty would need to prepare not just for the races themselves but for the high levels of competition he would face in each.

Each upcoming race was a new challenge, a test of how well Sovereignty could perform under the weight of expectations. The Preakness Stakes, being the second jewel in the Triple Crown, would bring a new set of competitors eager to dethrone the Kentucky Derby champion. Sovereignty, with his unassuming background, had already shown that he could handle pressure, but the Preakness would test his ability to continue winning against a field of horses who now saw him as the target. The challenge here would be to maintain his composure and focus. His victory in the Derby had made him a marked horse—every other competitor would be looking to beat him.

The Belmont Stakes, the final leg of the Triple Crown, presented another unique set of obstacles. Known for its longer distance and unique track conditions, it would demand even more from Sovereignty. The stamina required to run a longer race on a demanding track would test his endurance like never before. While Sovereignty had shown impressive speed and agility in the Derby, the Belmont would force him to tap into his reserves of strength, his mental toughness, and his ability to adapt to a new and challenging environment. For many horses, the Belmont is a race that can make or break their careers—Sovereignty's team knew that this would be a pivotal moment in his journey.

Beyond the Triple Crown races, Sovereignty's schedule would include other major competitions that would continue to build on his legacy. There were the prestigious Breeders' Cup races, known for bringing together the best horses from around the world, as well as international events in places like Europe and Dubai. These races would offer Sovereignty new challenges, as he faced some of the best horses from different racing cultures and track conditions. The opportunity to compete on an international stage would not only enhance his reputation but could also serve as a means to secure his place in history. The Breeders' Cup, in particular, would bring together the champions from all over the world, and a victory there could elevate Sovereignty's status to a global level.

However, the challenge of maintaining success in these races would not only be about racing against strong competitors but also about managing the increased scrutiny and expectations. After his Derby win, Sovereignty was no longer just another racehorse—he was the symbol of resilience, the underdog who had made it to the top. With that fame came the responsibility to continue proving himself. As the spotlight grew brighter, Sovereignty's team would need to carefully navigate his training, his recovery, and his mental preparation. Overcoming the challenge of external pressures and the psychological impact of being a champion was just as important as physical readiness.

In addition, there would always be the challenge of remaining injury-free. Horse racing is a physically demanding sport, and even the slightest injury could have a lasting impact on a horse's career. Sovereignty's team was committed to keeping him healthy, monitoring his every move to prevent overuse or injury. Preventative care, including regular check-ups, massages, and light training periods between races, was essential to ensure his longevity. The challenge of balancing the intensity of race preparation with the need for recovery would be one that Sovereignty's team would have to manage carefully.

As Sovereignty faced the challenges of the next races, his legacy was already beginning to take shape. He had proven that anything was possible, that a horse with a humble background could rise to the top and make history. However, his future races were a test of consistency. Each race was not just about another win but about proving that his Derby victory was no fluke, that he was capable of maintaining his status as one of the finest racehorses of his time. For Sovereignty, the road ahead was full of both opportunities and challenges, each race a new chapter in his journey to solidify his place in the annals of racing history.

Preparing for Retirement

As Sovereignty's career continued to flourish following his stunning 2025 Kentucky Derby victory, the conversation inevitably turned toward his eventual retirement. Every horse in racing reaches a point where their physical condition, stamina, and competitive drive no longer align with the demands of the track, and the question of when to retire becomes crucial for both the horse and their team. For Sovereignty, preparing for retirement was not simply about winding down; it was about making the transition with dignity and care, ensuring that his legacy as a champion was preserved while also setting him up for a comfortable and fulfilling life beyond racing.

The decision to retire Sovereignty would not be based on just one factor—it would involve a holistic assessment of his physical health, his mental state, and his ability to continue competing at the highest level. His team had already proven their dedication to ensuring his well-being, and this phase of his career would be no different. Retirement, after all, is a delicate transition, especially for a horse that had given so much to the sport. Sovereignty's future would need to be handled with the same care and attention to detail that had characterized his career from the beginning.

One of the most important considerations in preparing for Sovereignty's retirement was managing his physical health. Horse racing is a physically demanding sport, and over time, the wear and tear on a horse's body can accumulate, even for champions like Sovereignty. The team would begin monitoring his physical condition closely, watching for any signs of joint stress, muscle fatigue, or discomfort that might suggest it was time to call it a day. Sovereignty's health would be assessed through regular veterinary checkups, physical therapy, and non-invasive treatments such as massage therapy or acupuncture. The goal would be to ensure that Sovereignty's body was in the best possible condition for his final races and that when the time came to retire, he would be able to do so without any lingering injuries or pain.

Mental readiness for retirement was another key factor. Sovereignty had been a fighter from the start, and his tenacity and focus had helped him achieve greatness on the track. However, not every horse is emotionally prepared to transition from the intense, high-pressure world of competition to a quieter, more relaxed lifestyle. Sovereignty's team knew that retirement wouldn't just be about physical rest—it would also be about helping him adapt to a life away from the racetrack. The team would focus on creating an environment where Sovereignty could feel comfortable and content. This could involve giving him more time in pastures, allowing him to interact with other horses, and providing a space where he could rest and recover at his own pace. Keeping Sovereignty mentally engaged and happy was as important as preserving his physical health.

An essential aspect of preparing for Sovereignty's retirement was planning for his future after racing. For a horse of his stature, there would likely be multiple opportunities. One path could involve Sovereignty becoming a breeding stallion. As the winner of the Kentucky Derby, Sovereignty would carry significant value in the breeding world. His success on the track would make him an attractive prospect for breeding programs, and his bloodlines could potentially produce other champions. The team would need to make careful decisions about whether Sovereignty would enter the breeding program and how best to approach that transition. This would involve discussions with breeding farms, determining the best facilities for him, and ensuring that his transition from racehorse to stallion was as seamless and natural as possible.

On the other hand, there was the option of giving Sovereignty a peaceful retirement where he would live out his days without the pressures of breeding or racing. For many horses, this path is the most rewarding, allowing them to enjoy their golden years in comfort. Sovereignty could retire to a peaceful, well-maintained farm, where he could enjoy open spaces and the company of other retired racehorses. The key would be ensuring that Sovereignty's needs—whether physical, social, or mental—were met in this new phase of his life. Providing him with a quiet, peaceful life after the excitement of the racetrack could allow him to enjoy his time in retirement in a way that reflected the care and respect he had earned throughout his career.

Ultimately, the decision on Sovereignty's retirement would be made by his team, who had shown exceptional care and love for the horse throughout his career. Sovereignty had already proven that he was a true champion, not just in terms of his racing performance, but in his ability to overcome obstacles, to push through adversity, and to inspire those around him. His retirement, when it came, would be handled with the same thoughtfulness and respect that had defined every phase of his career. Sovereignty's legacy would be secure, whether he went on to sire future champions or lived out his days in peace, enjoying the tranquility of a life well-earned.

Chapter 12
The Legacy of an Underdog

Sovereignty's victory in the 2025 Kentucky Derby marked a turning point not only in his own career but in the way the world viewed the sport of horse racing. His rise from obscurity to Derby champion wasn't just a victory on the track; it was a statement—a testament to the strength of the underdog and the power of perseverance. Sovereignty's story became much more than a tale of racing. It resonated with a universal truth: greatness doesn't always come from privilege, and champions are often born from adversity rather than pedigree.

In the world of horse racing, where success has traditionally been tied to wealth, bloodlines, and sponsorships, Sovereignty's triumph represented a radical departure from the norm. For decades, racing had been a sport where the horses with the most prestigious bloodlines and the biggest financial backing were given the best chances for success. Sovereignty, with his modest pedigree and overlooked background, shattered that narrative. His victory symbolized the fact that the heart and determination of a horse, along with the commitment of those behind him, could be just as powerful as any inherited advantage.

Sovereignty's win had an immediate impact on the racing world. It forced industry leaders, trainers, and owners to reconsider what they valued in racehorses. While pedigree and investment had always been seen as key indicators of success, Sovereignty proved that even the underdogs could take center stage with the right combination of heart, resilience, and belief. For the first time in many years, horse racing became a sport where anyone — whether they were an established owner or a first-time trainer — could dream of winning the most prestigious race in the world, regardless of their financial resources or pedigree. Sovereignty was a symbol that opportunity was not reserved for the elite; it was a race open to anyone who had the will to compete.

But Sovereignty's legacy extends beyond the racing world. His story, one of perseverance and triumph against the odds, became a beacon for people everywhere who had ever been told they couldn't succeed. It was a powerful reminder that success doesn't come easily, and it's often the most unexpected individuals or horses who end up achieving greatness. Sovereignty showed the world that underdogs can rise above limitations and challenge the status quo. His story was a metaphor for all those who had been underestimated — those who had fought for their place in the world against overwhelming odds — and showed them that they too could defy expectations and carve their own path to success.

Sovereignty's influence also extended to the next generation of horses and trainers. Aspiring jockeys, owners, and young horses saw in Sovereignty the kind of success that can only come from hard work, determination, and a belief in one's abilities. His legacy sparked a wave of optimism and possibility, especially among those who had always seen racing as a sport dominated by financial power. Young trainers and horse owners, who might have once believed they could never compete with the established elite, now saw that they too had a place in the racing world. Sovereignty's victory was a rallying cry for these dreamers, a signal that with the right mindset, anything was possible.

One of the most profound aspects of Sovereignty's legacy lies in the way he challenged the myth of perfection. In a sport that often prizes the flawless pedigree and the polished appearance of the horses, Sovereignty represented the power of imperfection. He wasn't a horse born from the most prestigious bloodlines, nor did he come with the financial backing that many of his competitors had. But despite these perceived shortcomings, he proved that perfection was not a prerequisite for greatness. His success didn't come from being flawless—it came from his heart, his resilience, and his determination to prove that he belonged among the best. Sovereignty's story told the world that it's not about being perfect— it's about having the courage to face challenges head-on and the will to keep moving forward, even when the odds are stacked against you.

In many ways, Sovereignty became the embodiment of the power of imperfection. His journey was filled with struggles and doubts—yet each of those moments became part of what made his victory so remarkable. In an industry that often celebrated the idea of a perfect champion, Sovereignty's imperfections made him even more relatable and inspiring. He didn't come from a prestigious background, and he wasn't the fastest or most well-known. But in his imperfections, he found a kind of strength that no amount of money or pedigree could buy. His legacy became a celebration of the idea that greatness can emerge from imperfection, and that what matters most is not how you start but how you finish.

As Sovereignty's story continues to be told, it will undoubtedly serve as a source of inspiration for generations to come. His impact on the racing world is undeniable, but his influence stretches far beyond the track. Sovereignty's legacy is one of hope, resilience, and the belief that even the most unlikely candidates can rise to greatness. By rewriting the script on what it means to be a champion, he has left a lasting mark on the sport of horse racing—and on the hearts of all those who dare to dream. His journey proves that sometimes, the most extraordinary victories come from the most unlikely places.

Impact on the Racing World

Sovereignty's victory in the 2025 Kentucky Derby had a seismic impact on the horse racing world, altering the way the sport was perceived, both internally and externally. For decades, the narrative in racing had been firmly rooted in wealth, pedigree, and the ability to secure the best horses with the most elite bloodlines. Owners with deep pockets, prestigious stables, and access to the most influential trainers dominated the scene. But Sovereignty's victory, as an underdog with a modest pedigree and little financial backing, redefined those norms. He became a symbol of possibility, showing that greatness could emerge from the most unlikely places.

Prior to Sovereignty's Derby win, the racing world had come to believe that pedigree was the most crucial factor in a horse's potential for success. The sport had long been dictated by the idea that horses with the most illustrious bloodlines had the best chance of winning the most prestigious races, including the Kentucky Derby. The racing industry often emphasized this standard, shaping expectations around a horse's breeding and lineage rather than its inherent talent or heart. Sovereignty, however, demonstrated that while pedigree might offer advantages, it was not the sole determining factor for success.

Sovereignty's success challenged the very foundations of horse racing. His improbable rise to the top of the sport forced industry insiders—trainers, owners, and breeders alike—to reconsider their criteria for success. Pedigree, while still valuable, was no longer the sole determinant of a horse's future. The true qualities that led to Sovereignty's win—his heart, determination, and the unshakeable belief of his team—became a new standard. Trainers and owners began to rethink their strategies, focusing more on identifying horses with strong mental fortitude and physical resilience, rather than just relying on established bloodlines.

This shift had ripple effects across the entire industry. Suddenly, the dream of owning a champion racehorse didn't feel so out of reach for those without vast financial resources. Sovereignty's story empowered smaller owners and less affluent trainers to believe that with the right training, commitment, and strategy, they could compete at the highest levels. His victory inspired a new generation of racers and trainers, people who had previously felt sidelined by the elitism and high cost of the sport. Sovereignty's triumph showed them that success was no longer reserved for the ultra-wealthy and connected—it was now a sport where determination, grit, and the right team could take an underdog to the very top.

The media, too, played a critical role in magnifying Sovereignty's impact. The traditional media narrative of horse racing had always been dominated by the big names, the high-stakes sponsorships, and the horses with the most fame and fortune behind them. But Sovereignty changed all of that. His story captivated audiences around the world, and the media embraced his underdog narrative. For the first time in a long while, horse racing was a topic of mainstream conversation, not just among traditional fans but also among people who had never considered the sport. News outlets covered his story, documentaries were made, and social media buzzed with excitement. This newfound attention brought a level of public interest to the sport that it had not seen in years, helping to expand horse racing's fanbase and attract a new generation of enthusiasts.

The influence of Sovereignty's victory also extended to sponsorship and commercial opportunities. Before his win, the big sponsors typically gravitated toward high-profile horses owned by billionaires or those with flashy pedigrees. After his Derby win, companies began to recognize that the underdog story could resonate with a wider audience. Brands that had once overlooked the sport now saw the potential in aligning themselves with Sovereignty's success, particularly given the emotional connection he had built with fans. His victory showed that the sport was not only about luxury and prestige—it was about the triumph of the human (and equine) spirit, and that message resonated deeply with consumers across various demographics.

Moreover, Sovereignty's victory highlighted a shift in how the racing world approached the concept of talent identification. No longer would horses be defined solely by their bloodlines. The emphasis began to shift toward the training process, the mental fortitude of the horse, and the relationship between the horse and its handlers. Trainers began to take a more holistic approach to their horses, focusing not just on their physical speed and endurance, but also on their psychological resilience and emotional well-being.

Sovereignty had shown that a horse's ability to compete at the highest levels depended on more than just genetics—it depended on the strength of the bond between the horse and its team.

Sovereignty's legacy in the racing world was about more than just one race—it was about challenging the status quo and redefining what it meant to be a champion. His victory opened the door for horses with less-than-elite pedigrees, for smaller owners and trainers, and for anyone who believed that success in horse racing could be based on more than just wealth and lineage. Sovereignty's impact on the racing world was profound, proving that the sport could be about more than just a select few—it could be about resilience, heart, and the courage to defy expectations. In the years to come, his name would be remembered not only as the horse who won the 2025 Kentucky Derby, but as the one who changed the very nature of the sport, making it more inclusive, more inspiring, and more reflective of the power of the underdog.

Inspiring Future Generations

Sovereignty's improbable victory in the 2025 Kentucky Derby did more than just shake up the racing world—it inspired future generations of horse racing enthusiasts, trainers, owners, and young horses. His triumph is a beacon of hope and possibility for anyone who has ever been told they couldn't succeed, reminding the world that greatness isn't always determined by pedigree or wealth, but by determination, heart, and resilience. Sovereignty's story is one that will be told for years to come, not just in racing circles, but in broader cultural contexts, encouraging those from all walks of life to reach for their dreams, no matter how impossible they might seem.

For aspiring owners and trainers, Sovereignty's victory represented a shift in what was possible. Horse racing, long considered a sport for the elite, was now seen in a new light. His win proved that even the most modestly bred horses, without the financial backing of billionaires or the pedigrees of champions, could rise to the top. This opened the door for individuals who might have previously thought they had no chance in the sport. Sovereignty's journey—from an overlooked horse with limited resources to a Kentucky Derby winner—served as proof that perseverance, intelligent training, and a deep connection with the horse could result in success, regardless of starting point.

Young trainers and jockeys, many of whom had grown up watching the dominance of pedigreed horses, found new inspiration in Sovereignty's story. It gave them a reason to believe that their own ambitions were attainable. Rather than feeling confined to the sidelines because of financial or pedigree constraints, they were now empowered to dream bigger. Sovereignty showed that anyone with the right mindset and work ethic could make an impact, regardless of where they came from. The message that no dream was too big began to resonate with those entering the racing world, motivating them to pursue their passions with vigor, knowing that the potential for success was no longer reserved for the privileged few.

For the younger generation of racing fans, Sovereignty's story provided a much-needed shift in perspective. Horse racing, for many, had long been perceived as a sport dominated by the rich and powerful, with little room for outsiders to find success. But Sovereignty changed that narrative, showing fans that the sport was about more than just wealth and privilege. His victory made the sport more relatable, showing fans that anyone—regardless of background—could dream of victory at the highest level.

Sovereignty's win brought a fresh perspective to the sport, one that was inspiring, inclusive, and accessible.

Moreover, Sovereignty's legacy extended beyond the sport of horse racing itself. His story had universal appeal, transcending the world of horses and racing to touch on themes of perseverance, overcoming adversity, and challenging the status quo. He became a symbol of hope for anyone facing obstacles in their own lives, whether they were athletes, students, or individuals working to achieve their personal goals. Sovereignty proved that success doesn't require a perfect pedigree—it requires a willingness to fight against the odds, to believe in yourself when others doubt you, and to keep pushing forward, no matter the setbacks.

The impact on future generations of horses is also worth noting. Sovereignty's victory challenged the traditional criteria by which horses were judged. As his story became more widely known, breeders and trainers began to see the potential in horses that might not have come from elite bloodlines. The emphasis in the racing world began to shift more toward the individual talents and qualities of each horse, such as their personality, resilience, and ability to adapt. Sovereignty's legacy will likely lead to a more inclusive approach to horse breeding, where the focus is not solely on ancestry, but on the qualities that make each horse unique.

The future generations of horses racing after Sovereignty will feel the ripple effect of his achievement. His story will inspire new horses, trained and handled with the belief that they can also defy expectations and achieve greatness. Sovereignty has shown that racing is about more than just being fast—it's about the heart of the horse, the trust built between the horse and its team, and the courage to continue racing even when the odds are stacked against you.

As Sovereignty's name continues to echo through the annals of racing history, it will remain a source of inspiration for everyone involved in the sport—owners, trainers, jockeys, and fans alike. His legacy will endure as a reminder that true champions are not defined by their bloodlines or the size of their wallets, but by their spirit, determination, and the willingness to fight for what seems impossible. In the years to come, Sovereignty's influence will undoubtedly inspire future generations to chase their dreams, to race with all their heart, and to believe that, no matter where they start, they can reach the pinnacle of success. His story is one of hope, of defying the odds, and of creating a legacy that will inspire generations to come.

The Myth of Perfection and the Power of Imperfection

Sovereignty's victory in the 2025 Kentucky Derby not only disrupted the racing world but also challenged the long-held myth of perfection that has dominated the sport for decades. In a field where success is often measured by impeccable pedigrees, high financial investments, and flawless training, Sovereignty's triumph proved that imperfection could be just as powerful, if not more so. His story illuminated the fact that greatness doesn't require perfection—it requires heart, resilience, and the willingness to overcome obstacles, making him a symbol of how imperfection can lead to greatness.

In horse racing, the emphasis on perfection has been profound. Horses with the best bloodlines, owned by billionaires and trained by top-tier professionals, have long been seen as the most likely contenders for victory. The idea of a "perfect" horse—the one with the ideal genetic makeup, flawless technique, and an unbroken record of success—has shaped the way the industry defines champions. These horses are expected to perform without flaw, without the blemishes of inexperience, injury, or setbacks. In many ways, the sport has been about cultivating perfection, or at least the illusion of it.

However, Sovereignty's victory shattered this myth. He wasn't born from prestigious bloodlines, nor did he come from an elite background. His entry into the world of racing was marked by underestimation, skepticism, and doubt. He didn't fit the mold of the perfect racehorse—he had obstacles from the very beginning. But rather than being hindered by his perceived imperfections, Sovereignty thrived on them. His imperfections became his strength. He wasn't a horse groomed for greatness from the start; he was a horse who overcame adversity, defied expectations, and proved that success in racing wasn't about being perfect—it was about having the resilience to rise above the challenges.

Sovereignty's victory forced the racing world to confront the limitations of its obsession with perfection. It highlighted the fact that while pedigree, wealth, and flawless training are important, they are not the only factors that determine success. Sovereignty's win demonstrated that a horse's true potential comes from within— its heart, its ability to fight through adversity, and its willingness to continue competing even when the odds seem insurmountable. Sovereignty didn't fit the idealized version of a racehorse, but it was precisely because of his imperfections that he became a true champion. He didn't rely on perfection to get him to the top; he relied on his determination, his spirit, and his ability to push through when things didn't go as planned.

The power of imperfection in Sovereignty's story also lies in the way it inspired those who had been overlooked, dismissed, or told they couldn't succeed. Many aspiring trainers, owners, and jockeys in the racing world had grown accustomed to the idea that only the perfect horse could succeed—those with the best pedigree, the most money, and the most prestigious backers. But Sovereignty proved that this wasn't the only path to victory. His success showed that anyone, even those with humble beginnings, could defy the odds and rise to the top. His story resonated with people beyond the world of racing—it became a message to anyone who had ever been told they weren't good enough or didn't belong. Sovereignty's imperfections made him more relatable and accessible. His win was proof that talent, hard work, and heart could lead to greatness, even when the odds were stacked against you.

Furthermore, Sovereignty's legacy represents a more inclusive approach to the sport of horse racing. For years, racing had been dominated by horses with the perfect genetic blueprint, but Sovereignty's win showed that there's more than one way to achieve success. The industry began to shift, paying more attention to the horse as an individual, rather than just focusing on pedigree or wealth. Trainers started to appreciate the mental and emotional resilience that made a horse a champion, and the importance of developing a bond with the animal. This shift in focus from perfection to imperfection opened up opportunities for horses that might have previously been overlooked—those who might not have the "perfect" pedigree but had the heart and drive to succeed.

Sovereignty's victory also left a lasting impact on the way we view success in general. His story teaches us that perfection is a myth—no one, not even the best racehorses, can perform flawlessly all the time. Life, much like racing, is filled with imperfections, setbacks, and moments of doubt. But it is through these challenges that true character is built. Sovereignty's imperfections made his victory all the more extraordinary. His win was a reminder that greatness is not about being perfect; it's about persevering through the imperfections, learning from them, and continuing to fight for success, no matter the obstacles.

Sovereignty's legacy is a powerful reminder that the pursuit of perfection can often be limiting. His triumph proved that embracing imperfection can lead to a kind of greatness that is more enduring, more relatable, and more meaningful. By overcoming the myth of perfection, Sovereignty showed the world that the most powerful champions aren't necessarily the ones without flaws—but those who, despite their imperfections, find the strength to keep pushing forward and achieve the extraordinary.

www.ingramcontent.com/pod-product-compliance
Lightning Source LLC
LaVergne TN
LVHW061553070526
838199LV00077B/7029